The Golfer who Laughed

Phil Tresidder

THE GOLFER WHO LAUGHED

Illustrated by Mike Watkins

Stanley Paul
London Melbourne Sydney Auckland Johannesburg

Stanley Paul & Co. Ltd

An imprint of the Hutchinson Publishing Group

19–21 Conway Street, London W1P 6JD

Hutchinson Group (Australia) Pty Ltd
30–32 Cremorne Street, Richmond South, Victoria 3121
PO Box 151, Broadway, New South Wales 2007

Hutchinson Group (NZ) Ltd
32–34 View Road, PO Box 40–086, Glenfield, Auckland 10

Hutchinson Group (SA) (Pty) Ltd
PO Box 337, Bergvlei 2012, South Africa

First published 1982

© Phil Tresidder 1982

Printed by Graphic Consultants International Pte Ltd, Singapore

ISBN 0 09 137630 0

The Golfer Who Laughed

Of all the great characters thrown up by the game of golf, none could come within a fairway wood of Tommy Bolt, the stormy 'thunder-bolt' of the American tour. According to one chronicler, Bolt was Vesuvius. You never knew whether it was going to be a nice sunny day or the last days of Pompeii.

Bolt's club-wielding feats are legendary. They say he led the tour in twisted metal. When Bolt teed off the betting was not how few shots he would finish with but how few clubs.

Bolt came to the 18th one day in Florida and asked the caddie what club was required for a shot necessitating a 220-yard carry over water.

'A six-iron, sir', the caddie replied with an audible sigh.

'A six-iron?' Bolt exploded, his craggy face turning a deep shade of purple. 'Why, it's 240 yards to the flag. How can it be a six-iron?'

'Because that's all you have left in the bag', the boy answered.

Such are the legendary and greedily devoured, if apocryphal, stories that surround the incorrigible old trouper.

Other players held records for longest drives; Bolt held records for longest drivers. He threw one into a pond at Cherry Hills, in Denver, in the American Open one year. An observer claimed that if it had been a discus Bolt would have won the Olympics, though others suggested the Denver altitude was a factor.

Once, Bolt had to pay a deep-sea diver $75 to swim down a canal and rescue his favourite driver from twenty fathoms.

The Professional Golfers Association later put Tommy in charge of the tour's 'good conduct' committee which, according to one sceptic, was a little like putting the rabbit in charge of the lettuce or the fox in charge of the chicken coop. Tommy, honesty personified, duly fined himself $100 for club throwing.

Yes, old Thunder blew his top, too, on more than one visit to Australia. He always maintained if, instead of being cast as the villain, the crowds had cheered for him, he would have consistently fired in the low 60s. 'It's my face, don't you see?' he said. 'I got this big lantern jaw, and my face gets red and all. Now, you take these baby-faced, flippy-wristed kids they got today, and it don't show when they get mad. Don't you see?'

Tommy Bolt duly carried off the Australian Seniors crown at Manly Club on the northern Sydney coastline. During the final round, he asked one of the gallery how he was faring in the tournament scores. 'You're out in front and daylight's coming second', the fan joked back. Bolt scratched his head and asked the gallery, 'Now who the hell is this guy Daylight?'

It was at Manly that the one and only Tommy Bolt was heard to call on the Lord to damn and commit to eternal hellfire a particular bunker that had spoilt his round. 'And don't send your Son down. This is a man's job', he growled.

The American professional, Hubert Green (yes, he's so superstitious he wears green ensembles in regular tournament play) is a stickler for the rules — even during the 1979 Masters at Augusta when a deadly three-foot water moccasin headed towards American PGA president, Frank Cardi.

Said a cautious Green, 'If I swing at that snake chasing you, Frank, you won't penalize me for grounding a club in a hazard?'

Frank Cardi screamed back, 'No—kill it, kill it'.

Hubert performed the execution with five swings of a two-iron. Other players observing the drama said Green's club choice was poor. The leading edge of a wedge would have produced a neater result, they agreed.

An extract from a West Country (England) golf bulletin:

'As in previous years, the evening concluded with a toast to the new president in champagne provided by the retiring president, drunk as usual at midnight.'

Isao Aoki, a sports hero in golf-nutty Japan, has reason to enjoy his sojourns in Britain. Tall for a Japanese (he's a six-footer) and famous for his unorthodox putting in which he rests the heel of the putter head on the turf and the toe up in the air, he won the world match-play championship at the Wentworth course, outside London. He failed to win in a subsequent year but compensated with a spectacular hole-in-one, bouncing a seven-iron into the cup for the richest prize in history. He won a luxury home and furnishings worth $120,000 near the famous Gleneagles course in Scotland. Aoki's English is poor. But he said it all when he announced, 'U.K...O.K.'.

The American professional, Charles Coody, was philosophical about his indifferent form. He said, poker-faced, 'I'm hitting my drives badly, my iron play is erratic and the putts are just not falling in. Other than that, everything is just fine.'

Carol Mann, winner of more than $500,000, is one of the great personalities of the American Ladies professional tour. She has even won a place in golf's Hall of Fame.

Carol's other claim to fame is that she is the tallest player on tour, standing a towering six feet three inches. Is she sensitive about her lofty station? Not at all.

'I am five feet fifteen inches tall', she says with a grin.

Ronnie Corbett, the English comedian, stands five feet one inch, which means he is about eyeball height to a wedge.

A golfing nut, Corbett turned out for a pro-am tournament in Sydney wearing an outsized tam o'shanter. 'It's a BBC tartan tam o'shanter, really', he quipped. 'Small cheques.'

Corbett told his gallery, 'I don't mind being funny twenty-four hours a day and I love making people laugh, but I get sick of being little the whole time'.

'Whoops ... the old unlucky 13th again.'

Two Americans, playing the Australian Club layout, Kensington, for the first time were puzzled by a marker that read '458 metres'.

One inquired, 'What's the difference between yards and metres?'

The other responded doubtfully, 'Really, I don't know. But I think when it's in metres, you just hit it a little harder.'

Australian Broadcasting Commission commentators during the national PGA championship at Royal Melbourne tried faithfully to keep viewers briefed in metric measurements.

When Bob Shearer's putt came to rest alongside the cup, the commentator revealed it had missed by 12.5 millimetres.

Another commentator told viewers that a player faced a putt of a metre. But when the ball rolled boldly beyond the cup, the commentator exclaimed that it had missed 'by miles'.

Al Geiberger, a forty-three-year-old Californian, has a special place in international golf's record books. In 1977, he carded a 59 in the second round of the Danny Thomas Memphis Classic that included eleven birdies, one eagle and six pars. His barrier-breaking achievement hit world headlines.

Geiberger gave interviewers this little insight to homelife and his future as an ageing professional. 'Our sons have set up a little golf course in the backyard and all the neighbours' kids come over. They play tournaments and instead of using their own names, pick favourites from the tour. So far someone has always taken me. When the day comes that I'm not in their tourney, I'll know it is time to quit.'

There are all sorts of golfing victims around the world but Geraldton jockey, Trevor Davis, once provided his own unique tale of woe.

Davis was riding the odds-on favourite, Salako, at the

Utakarra racecourse about 400 kilometres from Perth.

His mount was travelling beautifully shortly after the start and, with only two other horses in the race, Davis had already started to speculate what he would do with his earnings from the winning ride. Then, whack!... he was hit on the head by a golf ball. Needless to say, the local golf course is next door to the track.

'I was hit just below the right eye — I couldn't believe it', he recalled.

But the story had a happy ending. Salako proved too strong and went on to win by three lengths. Oh yes, and the jockey wasn't seriously hurt.

The *Sydney Morning Herald* listed the results of a day's play in the Australia-Japan golf trophy series at Royal Canberra in their judo details column!

Australian golfer, Noel Ratcliffe, reckoned he was neatly 'conned' when he played a practice round with the great Argentinian trouper, Roberto de Vicenzo, on the eve of a British Open.

About to drive off around a dog — leg par four with tall trees in the corner—Ratcliffe heard Roberto say, 'When I was your age I used to drive the ball over those trees'.

Ratcliffe took the bait and launched a big hit intended to clear the trees. The ball didn't make it and fell with a clunk into the rough.

'But when I was your age, those trees had only just been planted', said Roberto, putting a kindly hand on the Australian's shoulder.

So you reckon fishermen spin tall tales. Well, what about this Queensland golfer for putting them in their place?

William Crowther, playing the Carbrook course at Southport, mis-hit a shot to the 8th green and the ball lobbed into the nearby Logan River.

The ball landed squarely on the head of a two-pound bream. Mr Crowther retrieved the stunned fish and ate it for lunch.

Reader's Digest magazine delved into the world of golf to list the worst played golf hole. This is the magazine's description:

'Her name is lost in history but the woman who finished last in the 1912 Shawnee Invitational for Ladies in Pennsylvania will live for ever. When she teed off the 16th hole her drive went directly into a nearby river. She gamely set out in a rowing boat to play the ball. When she finally succeeded in striking it out of the water, it landed in dense woods. From there she drove the ball into the rough, then into a sand trap, then back into the rough. Her final score for the hole was 166!'

Jack Nicklaus is the greatest golfer who ever lived. Nobody would dispute that, except tour player Fred Marti who, in a light-hearted moment, chided the Golden Bear, 'You're not so damned good, you know. You've just been on a lucky thirteen-year streak!'

A golfer asked his professional, aged seventy-two, for a lesson.

'Yes', replied the old pro, 'I can manage it in the morning, but I'm sorry I can't help out in the afternoon, as I've got to go and see my father'.

'Your father?' asked the golfer incredulously. 'How old is he then?'

'He's ninety-five', replied the professional.

'And does he play golf, too?'

'Well', replied the pro, 'he knocks the ball round a bit but he'll never make a player'.

Walter Hagen was the cavalier of golf, a handsome six-footer with slick black hair and a huge appetite for life. More than once he arrived at the first tee, straight from an all-night party and still exuding the aroma of whisky and cigars.

Hagen summed up his outlook to life in these immortal lines, 'You're only here for a short time. Relax. Stop to smell the flowers along the way.'

On one occasion, Hagen faced a tough tournament encounter and a friend was astonished to see him up late and enjoying himself.

'Why aren't you in bed, Walter?' the friend asked. 'Don't you know that your opponent has been in bed for hours?'

'Yeah', drawled Walter, 'but is he asleep?'

British Customs at London's Heathrow Airport were on the alert when they spotted a box labelled 'Assault with a deadly weapon'. They found the box contained nothing more lethal than advertising literature for Greenirons, a California-based golf-club manufacturer. The 'assault' line is their slogan.

For some reason, manufacturers have introduced a more savage note into the club-naming field. For a long time the emphasis was on status — the Hogan Director, Spalding Executive, Macgregor VIP, Wilson Staff...

But at the Merchandise Show at Disney near Orlando, club names included Lynx, Tigress and Cobra, and perhaps the most primitively savage of them all — The Tiger Shark.

No doubt about it, Arthur D'Arcy (Bobby) Locke presented a venerable, squire-like figure in his baggy plus-fours, white eye-shade and Royal and Ancient tie tucked between the buttons of a white business shirt that encompassed a generous tummy spread.'Old Muffin Face' they called him and the galleries loved the genial old-world South African who, during World War II, flew more than 100 missions for the Allies over enemy territory. He came to Australia in 1938 as a lithe, athletic young fellow but when he retired in 1951, war service and a share of the good life that followed had transformed him into a heavy-jowled man and the most unlikely sports champion one might ever expect to meet.

Bobby Locke played with a casual 'banana-like' hook and he conceded much distance on the fairways to the young power-hitting lions. But once on the greens, he regularly spanked their backsides, holing wondrous putts with a magic putting stroke first moulded on the wiry kikuyu surfaces of his homeland where he practised for hours at a time, often at night under the reflected lights of the clubhouse. He won thirteen United States tour events and the Yanks finally found a technicality to ease him out of their circuit and prize-money.

Nothing could hurry Bobby Locke on the golf course. He was the original slow-poke. But just once his jovial humour was ruffled. He heard a man in the gallery announce loudly to a friend, 'There's that slow old man from South Africa'. Locke, thirty years of age, bristled at the 'old' even if he took less umbrage at the 'slow'. He turned, singled out the spectator and asked him, 'How old do you think I am?' The spectator replied, 'Oh, about forty'. Locke answered peevishly, 'Well, you're ten years out'. The spectator rejoined, 'What, fifty!'

You might reckon the golfer who bought 150 pairs of socks was set up for life. It actually happened to Gene Sarazen, the swarthy little American champion of yesteryear, as easily identified by his knickers as Ben Hogan by his flat white cap, Bobby Locke by his ageing tie and Kel Nagle by his panama.

Sarazen, who came to Australia several times and in 1936 carried off our Open championship, was the first player to complete the Grand Slam of the world's four major championships. Knickers were Sarazen's trademark. Despite a stocky, rotund figure he was always elegantly turned out in his plus-fours, knee-length socks, cap and matching accessories. Indeed, he wore knickers as far back as 1919 when he broke into golf as a seventeen-year-old and he never deviated from the style while winning seven major championships.

'Everybody was wearing knickers in 1919', he recalled. 'Walter Hagen, the greatest competitor golf ever had, led the parade. He had them tailor-made with his name around the kneeband. But when knickers went out in the 1930s I kept wearing 'em.

'With me it was strictly a practical thing. I'm only five feet five inches and very thick-bodied. If I wore slacks, they'd wrap around my knees at the top of my swing. Of course, with knickers, you had to wear long socks or you'd look like an idiot. The real long socks went out with the knickers.

'I remember a Pittsburgh salesman back in the late 1930s who decided the socks were going to come back in style and he went over to Scotland and bought 5,000 pairs at about $10 a pair. But his store couldn't move 'em. Nobody wanted them any more. He finally offered me a deal at 75 cents a pair and I bought 150 pairs.'

When the handsome young Spaniard, Severiano Ballesteros, won the British Open, the Spanish sherry industry put down a 110-gallon cask of sherry in one of the ancient sherry bodegas in Jerez, in Southern Spain. It took its place alongside casks dedicated to and signed by Napoleon, Wellington and Sir Winston Churchill.

Ballesteros, who signed a cool half-million dollar contract with Dunlop after his triumph, has astonished purists with his death-or-glory, often wayward power hitting. With his spectacular 'lasso' finish, Ballesteros whips the clubhead through at about 150 mph, while most golfers average around 120 mph. On his way to victory in the British Open, he succeeded in hitting only two fairways during the final thirty-six holes and once actually played from a carpark to register a birdie.

Seve's motto is clearly, 'Hit it hard, go and find it, hit it hard again'.

Son of a Spanish farmer, he carried golfbags as a youngster for a fistful of pesetas. At twenty-two years of age he became the youngest ever winner of the British Open and a millionaire overnight. He can balance eight golf balls in the palm of one of those powerful, olive-skinned hands. Superstitious, he will not play in competition with a golf ball with Number Three markings on it. He says it psychs him into three-putting!

When a critic chided him for his seemingly reckless play, Ballesteros countered by recalling that he had missed one 'cut' in the United States Open because he had tried to play too safely and conservatively. 'I'm like a racing car capable of hitting 250 mph', he said with an engaging grin. 'I go best with my foot down.'

Golf is not always the deadly grim and serious business dead-pan professionals might have you believe as they putt before hushed spectators across slippery, treacherous greens. There is a zany side to the game and a shoal of novel, bizarre achievements in the record books. Golfers have hit golf balls off wooden pegs held in the clenched teeth of delectable lady partners. A golfer once holed-in-one after hitting the ball off the face of his watch. Golf balls have been hit out of a bottle, from the bottom of a rowing boat, off clubhouse roofs, out of tree branches and, yes, even off the moon's surface.

Captain Alan B. Shepard struck the first extraterrestrial golf ball on 6 February 1971 with a six-iron during Apollo XIV's mission. We are told that Shepard swung with only his right hand and sent the first ball 200 yards, thanks to the moon's weak gravitational force. He promptly shanked a second six-iron shot! The clubhead was custom made and clipped onto the end of a rock-collecting implement. In 1974, Shepard gave the club to the United States Golf Association, where it is encased in Golf House's trophy room.

In the misty year of 1876 David Strath backed himself to go round St Andrews under 100 in moonlight. He took 95 and, moreover, did not lose a ball. But he was upstaged by Rufus Stewart, the Kooyonga, Adelaide, professional who, in 1931, went round his home course at night in 77, using only a torch shone by a friend to see the ball. This remarkable round lasted only one and three-quarter hours and he required only one ball, which is on display, without a dent or a cut, in the Kooyonga clubhouse.

But for sheer athleticism, nothing can beat Ian Colston who, in November 1971, played 401 holes in twenty-four hours at Bendigo Golf Club. The Bendigo course yardage was reduced to 6061 to conform to the minimum 6000 yards required for such records. Colston's friends illuminated the course with car lights during darkness. He sprinted between holes wearing a singlet and shorts throughout.

And if you think that everything is biggest and best in Texas, well a bunch of forty-three golfers from Antil Park Country Club, Picton, (New South Wales) toppled the fastest ever 18-hole record of 10 minutes 11.4 seconds set by Texan golfers. The Australians were stationed at strategic spots around the course and they whipped through the round in just 9 minutes 19.5 seconds. Proceeds from their feat went to guide dogs for the blind.

Golf's most famous hustler is reported to be a gentleman by the name of A.C. Thompson who took his place in American golf's folklore as 'Titanic Thompson'. How did he get his nickname? Apparently, when the chips were down and the pigeons 'hooked', he could sink the unsinkable on the putting greens.

Golfers who met him subsequently tried to outdo each other in colourful stories about his exploits. He was a talented

'I knew he'd never get out of there with his sand iron.'

player, of course, but he turned his back on meagre tournament purses, preferring to use his skills to better advantage in the business of hustling.

A golfer who knew him well related this incident: 'Titanic once made a boast he could drive a ball 500 yards. The reaction was exactly what he expected — money on the barrelhead. When the pile was high enough — about $10,000 — they all drove out to a course near a lake on a cold winter's day. When he picked out a tee near the edge of the lake his suckers knew they were doomed. His long straight drive hit the frozen surface of the lake and was still travelling when the bets were paid off.'

Sir Leslie Herron, the late Chief Justice, was in his day a golfer of great enthusiasm. For many years, he was president of the Australian Golf Club, Kensington, and it was in this capacity on one occasion that he welcomed professional competitors to a major tournament sponsored by a leading wine company. Sir Leslie told the assembled guests at the tournament-eve cocktail party, 'Now, I can't say that I have ever tried these particular wines, but I can tell you I have tried plenty who have'.

Jack Nicklaus remarked, 'You answer questions a lot differently when you're thirty-nine than when you were twenty-five. At twenty-five, I was brutally honest. At thirty-nine, I'm carefully honest.'

Honest he was when he related events during a United States Open championship. Nicklaus hit his tee shot on to the fairway at the 13th hole, hurried to a nearby portable toilet, came back to triple bogey the hole and promptly faded from contention.

In the pressroom afterwards he said, 'I don't know how this is going to look in print but I never did get my mind back on what I was doing after I went to the toilet'.

Was he sorry he went? 'No', he said, 'I had to go'.

Sam Snead, a golfing legend in his own time, caddied as a boy barefoot in the snow because shoes were something you saved for school and churchgoing. Snead never quite shed his hill-billy image, nor did he really want to. He was proud of his struggle as a raw-boned youngster from the foothills of West Virginia to golfing stardom. His swing is renowned as the most relaxed, the most fluent and the most beautiful in the whole world of big golf. Galleries still revere his presence on the circuit and in the 1979 Quad Cities tournament he fired rounds of 67-66 to equal, then better, his age.

His manager and life-long friend, the late Fred Corcoran, once wrote that if Walter Hagen was the first golfer to make a million dollars and spend it, then Sam Snead was the first to make a million — and save two million. Sam's legendary thrift is the source of some of the game's greatest stories.

Asked by a curious media what he did with all his money, Snead replied that he hid it away in jam jars in his backyard. The joke backfired when he returned from a tournament and found his backyard completely dug up by fortune hunters.

The media loved Snead and highly prized 'Sneadisms' that, in turn, delighted the American sports fans. Snead, for his part, enjoyed his hillbilly role and contributed to the stories with his own fertile imagination. Corcoran approached him at the 10th hole of a tournament during the 1948 presidential election and told him Dewey was leading. Sam solemnly digested the news and then replied, 'What did he get out in?' And when Corcoran urged Snead to send a congratulatory cable to Bing Crosby, who had won an Academy award for *Going My Way*, Sam gave a laconic, 'Okay ... did he win at match or medal play?'

Golf followers for decades have associated Snead with his range of straw hats. As Corcoran put it, the hat has become a sort of a uniform, covering a dome that has been a source of dismay and embarrassment to Sam. While the more exuberant pros might dance a jig and fling their hats in the air on the 72nd green, certainly not Sam. His hat has always remained firmly glued to his brow, and there is a popular suspicion that he wears it to bed. Corcoran once had a photograph taken of Sam in Florida showing him getting a haircut with his hat on! But the manager said he could vouch for the fact that he removes it in the shower, in church, at the dinner-table and in bed.

Probably Corcoran's most humorous anecdote concerned a tournament at Belmont where Sam shared a hotel room with another pro, Johnny Bulla. Recalled Corcoran:

'Their room was next to mine and I was awakened every morning by a peculiar thumping sound, as if something was being rolled or bumped across the floor. At the same time I noticed Sam was wearing automobile tape wrappings on both wrists. Finally I sought out Bulla and asked him for enlightenment.

"I know it's silly", said Johnny, "but he's walking on his hands to make his hair grow. Something about the blood rushing to the scalp and stimulating the follicles ..." '

Snead continued his search for the elixir of hair life — 'the greatest one-man quest since Galahad and Ponce de Leon turned in their cards'. Years later, Corcoran mentioned his name as he sat in a barber's chair in the Savoy Plaza, in New York. The barber's shears stopped snipping and he stared off into space.

'Where 'ave I 'eard dat name?', he mused.

Corcoran told him, 'Well, he's one of the greatest golfers in the world and he usually stops here when he's in town'.

The barber waggled his comb and said, 'Ah, now I know... a bell is ring' up 'ere'. He stepped over to a shelf and picked up a bottle of hair tonic. 'We just mailed 'im six bottles of dis hair tonic', he smiled. 'He think maybe it mak' 'is 'air grow.'

There was never any doubt that Dave Hill, an American tour firebrand, would have a bestseller on his hands when he pushed the clubs aside for a moment and tackled the typewriter keys. Outspoken and contentious, he once drew the wrath of Golf Association officials by claiming the fairways of a U.S. Open venue should be dug up and sown with corn.

Hill pulled no punches in his candid book called *Teed Off*. He tossed these broadsides at four of his contemporaries.

GARY PLAYER 'He works harder at golf than the rest of us — as he is always telling anyone who will listen, especially the writers.

'Gary is a little man and he's tremendously proud of his superior physical condition. He runs and lifts weights and eats health foods. That's all well and good, but I get tired of hearing him brag about it. So what if he has the most perfect bowel movement on the tour?'

TOM WEISKOPF 'Tom has always had the mechanical game to challenge Nicklaus, but you have to wonder if he'll ever grow up. He's spoiled and conceited and thinks everything should go exactly the way he wants it to. He reminds me of a kid I used to play marbles with. When he couldn't win he'd pick up his marbles and go home.'

HUBERT GREEN 'He's cocky and something of a smart-aleck. He likes to play too fast. Slow him down and he's less effective. His game isn't much to look at. His swing is quick and too upright and he dips his shoulder coming down into the ball. Putting, he splits his hands on the shaft, spreads his legs, and hankers over the ball like a chicken laying an egg.'

BILLY CASPER 'He has as much personality as a glass of water. Billy may think religion has helped his golf, but you have to be confused in the first place to think that religion will help you hit a better golf shot. That's like a Catholic fighter crossing himself coming into the ring. It's great if he can fight.'

Tom Watson, quietly-spoken winner of three British Opens and the heir to the Nicklaus throne, has explained why he has such an effective short game.

'When I was a kid, I practised chipping and putting all the time', he recounted. 'I didn't practise driving because I was afraid I'd lose the ball. Losing a golf ball when you don't have many and don't know when or where or how you're going to get another, well, it can just make you sit down and cry.'

'Drive for show, putt for dough', is golf's oldest maxim. Nobody contests that it is on the greens that championships and titles are won and lost, nevertheless there is unashamed gallery admiration for the fellow who can step up and clout the mammoth drive.

George Bell, the strong-arm, muscular Sydney professional was peerless as a long hitter during his best years. Contesting the annual King of the River driving contest across the Nepean River at Penrith, New South Wales, he used a two-wood to carry the ball 319 yards in 1971. He drove off a coir mat on the back of a truck. Bell has many hits of more than 400 yards to his credit and one, reportedly, of 550 yards at St Michael's Club in Sydney.

For the statistics freaks, an Australian meteorologist, Nils Lied, claimed in 1962 that he drove a ball 2,640 yards across ice at Mawson Base, Antartica.

The Americans stage a national long driving championship each year. Strictly supervised, Evan ('Big Cat') Williams holds the record with a blow of 353 yards 2 feet in 1977. Big Cat Williams had his golf bag inscribed 'Long Driving Champion'. A woman in an airport queue noticed the bag and asked Williams, 'Do you know Mario Andretti?'

If the Scots discovered golf (disputed by the Dutch), then it needed the Irish to give the game both humour and character.

Peter Dobereiner, a British scribe of rare wit and perception for the game, made a golfing pilgrimage to Ireland and began his account of the trip for his London *Observer* readers with this story:

'I was having a quiet drink in a Cork pub one evening wearing my flasher mac, when a man standing next to me suddenly shouted, "Christ! It's Ian Paisley!"'

'The events of the ensuing few minutes returned with total recall as the Belfast shuttle plonked down at Aldergrove, for I was headed on a brief visit to Paisley's constituency and painfully aware that Northern Ireland was a country of two communities in the thrall of clerics. Or had been. Was it still true?

'Naturally, I put the question to a senior Ulster theologian. The holy man paused in his labours of polishing the altar and straightening the beer mats, and busied himself with a curious alchemy involving Bushmills and hot water while he considered the question. "Yes, you could say that we are two communities."

'He led me to the window of his sacristy, on the first floor of the Royal Portrush Golf Club, and pointed to the wild duneland across Dunluce links. "One half of the population of Northern Ireland was conceived in those dunes", he said, "and the other half did their basic conceptual training in the same dunes. 'Tis frightful sad."

"Sad?"

'He fixed me with a stare of religious fervour. "Sad, indeed. We're getting terrible coastal erosion. We're in danger of losing the 5th green altogether and that's a grand hole."

"You mean ....?"

"Windblow", he added darkly, and I left it at that.'

The very soul of Irish golf is reflected in Christy O'Connor, the most famous professional ever to come out of the Shamrock Isle. He was born beside the first tee at Salthill, Galway, in 1924. One critic would query that, alleging he

'He says he's over here to buy a set of golf clubs ... Yarra Yarra, Manly, Royal Adelaide.'

wasn't born at all, but was hewn from a granite quarry.

Over a span of thirty years or so, he won everything worth winning in the British Isles except the Open and, in 1965, he missed that by only a shot. He was a self-confessed hell-raiser in his prime with an unashamed thirst for the old Guinness. The Irish revered him. They called him 'Himself'.

O'Connor speaks in a brogue as soft as an Irish mist. He gave this account of his early struggle for fame and recognition.

'The 1940s, just after the War — now that was a terrible time for a young man from the west of Ireland trying to make a living with nothing but a second-hand bag of clubs and a fierce desire to come face to face with Henry Cotton or Ben Hogan.

'Ah, sure I had confidence and certainty of youth in those days. I knew I could beat them all — if only I could get at them.

'I had a dream and worked hard at my game. I had no one to teach me. My first job was on a little nine-hole club at Cong, Co. Mayo. I used to cut the greens and look after the course and, when I'd finish work, I'd give a few lessons.

'After a few months I moved on to another nine-hole course at Tuam, not far from Galway City. From there I used to travel around the west of Ireland giving lessons for half a crown a time, trying to scrape up enough cash to get on the English tour. It was hard work trying to hang on to a quid. I'd get to a little town like Mullingar on Monday, then work up a thirst giving lessons at the local club and play a couple of rounds with the local parish priest (he was always good for a meal). By the end of the week, I'd be great friends with everybody from the local butcher to the greenkeeper's dog. By the time it came to leave most of my hard-earned half-crowns had found their way back into the coffers of the local pub.

'Anyway I got back to my digs one day to find a letter from Fred Daly inviting me to play in a tournament at Belfast; he had enclosed a return train ticket — which was just as well as I was down to my last two bob. Now, you can imagine my excitement at getting an invitation from the likes of Fred Daly. He was not just one of my heroes but, that very year, had become the first and unfortunately the last Irishman ever to win the British Open.

'It was my first tournament and I can tell you I was shaking like a leaf when I teed up. But there must have been a few players coming from somewhere because, after 72 holes, I had won by two shots from Harry Bradshaw. They presented me with a cup and fifty guineas.

'I can't remember much about the next few days except to say I don't know which I lost first — the cup or my last guinea. It must have been a great time because Guinness in those days was a shilling a pint and cigarettes were ten pence a packet.

'Four days later, some of my new friends put me on the train to Tuam. By some miracle I still had my return ticket but not much else. I had a pint of Guinness and a couple of sandwiches on the train and, when I got off at Tuam, I had one shilling and threepence left. So, instead of going back to my lodgings where I knew I would be slightly embarrassed, I bought a ticket for the local cinema and slept for six hours — at that stage I don't think I'd been to bed for four days.

'Sure, everyone thought I was mad and, looking back on it after all these years, I probably was ... just a little.'

Asked whether he ever felt annoyed by pressmen who refer to him as 'Himself' and 'Wristy Christy', he smiled indulgently. Then he said, 'I'll only ever get annoyed if they start calling me "Herself" '.

'I've got my golf game and my sex life all mixed up. I'm hooking during the day and fading at night.'

The quote could only come from American Doug Sanders, playboy, peacock dresser, extrovert and golfer supreme. He missed winning the British Open by a tiddler putt.

Sanders says he has no regrets about burning the midnight oil in his hey-day. 'I'd do the same thing again. I've lived one of the greatest lives of anyone. Frank Sinatra said to me once that only a few of us have done it our way. Would I have been more successful if I'd dedicated myself? Probably, but that's me. I calculate my wealth by my friends and I'm as wealthy as any man there is.'

What did other players think? Gary Player opined, 'If he had lived just an abnormal life he would have won twice as many tournaments'.

You'd have to admit that Lee Trevino, golf's 'Merry Mex', has got his priorities in life right. Each morning he hangs himself behind the door, face downwards inside a special contraption he has constructed to stretch his troublesome back.

Trevino confides, 'A lot of people think all the professionals get bad backs from the stress and strain of hitting balls. It's also from lifting luggage from the trunk of your car and at airports. That's why I have a road manager with me to do all that stuff. If it's heavier than a twelve-ounce can of beer, I won't pick it up.'

The little South African golfing gamecock, Gary Player, is rarely lost for words. But wife Vivienne, an excellent golfer herself, left him speechless when she tackled a par-three course in Johannesburg. Vivienne played four holes in 1-1-2-3.

Gary said, 'She hit a five-iron straight into one cup. On the next hole she knocked a six-iron straight into the hole and on the following green, I swear, her shot stopped just six inches from the front of the hole'.

Vivienne turned to her famous golfing husband and said, 'Top that!'

Grantland Rice, perhaps America's most versatile and prolific sports writer, was on the scene when golf was starting to win popularity. But this strange Scottish game didn't make any impact with his sports editor, Francis Albertanti, who disparaged its importance.

Albertanti, according to Rice, hailed from the lower East Side. He knew fights — and how to publicize them. In fact, he later became Tex Rickard's press agent. But in Albertanti's book, golf was something played by unemployed sheepherders and 'coupon-clipping' stiffs. It didn't belong on the sports pages.

Theophilus England Niles, the *Mail*'s managing editor, called Albertanti into his office one day to ask why golf wasn't receiving space.

'Golf? What's golf?' asked Francis.

'Why, it's a game — an important game', replied Niles. 'A lot of big businessmen are playing it.'

'Then put it on the financial page', retorted Albertanti.

If ever there was a rags to riches story in golf, it belongs to Gary Player, son of a Johannesburg coal miner, who is one of the game's playing millionaires today. You could set your clock by his annual visits to Australia — his seven Australian Open titles are a record achievement.

Closely associated with the Player success story is a Johannesburg businessman, George Blumberg, who first set eyes on the youngster from his window high in a block of flats in the suburb of Killarney. Young Player was practising that morning when George Blumberg went off to his factory and he was still practising when George Blumberg returned that evening. Immensely impressed by such dedication, Blumberg invited Gary to tea, a friendship sprang up and George contributed to Gary's first overseas tour expenses. They made many tours together subsequently.

Player recounts in his book, *Grand Slam Golf* : 'Each time I meet George in a hotel or at an airport or in any public place, I always have to ask him for a dollar or a shilling for a taxi or the porter. I seldom carry money with me, preferring to pay by cheque or by credit card, and this has led to a lot of fun and games between George and me.

'A few years back, George was sitting having a drink with Arnold Palmer when Arnold said, "I wish you would speak to Muff, George" (Palmer calls me Muff). "I've been travelling all over with him, and he is always asking me for dollars and quarters. Now you know Gary can have anything he wants from me, but this whole business is beginning to irritate me."

'George immediately got up and came across the room to where I was sitting and told me all this, and I said, "Isn't that awful, George, how much do you think I owe Arnold?" George said, "Well, Arnold says it must be $100." So I put out my hand and said, "George, lend me $100". Without thinking George gave me the money and I walked over and paid Arnold.'

Arnold Palmer, the critics concede, gave big golf a new dimension. The undisputed king, he brought a rugged charm to the game and a panache that had the galleries roaring in his wake. 'Arnie's armies' they called them.

Then along came Jack Nicklaus to wrest the crown from Arnold. The famous pair came under the same management, travelled together and became firm friends, although their rivalry remained fierce.

Nicklaus took time to win over the galleries and he admits to this day that he lacks some of the crowd-appeal qualities of Palmer, who is ten years his senior. 'When Arnie hitches up his trousers on a putting green', said Jack of Palmer, 'the crowd goes "oooohhh". They don't watch me if I hitch up my pants.'

Arnie's pants-hitching has been his trademark out on the course. It once prompted a sixteen-year-old, Mike Bradley from Florida, to do a bit of research. He followed Palmer and counted the number of hitches during a round of a tournament and the tugs amounted to 345.

Arnie won the tournament and afterwards explained to teenager Mike: 'The reason I hitch my trousers goes back to a time when I was about your age. My hips were always sort of narrow and my pants had a tendency to slide down. My mother was always on at me saying, "Arnold, tuck your shirttail in". So in order to please her, I started pulling 'em up all the time. I've done it so long now that I'm totally unconscious of even doing it.'

Old trouper Sam Snead's astonishing fitness and flexibility is a byword in the game of golf. His great parlour trick was to touch the top of a door with his foot in a sort of backflip. On the eve of each year's Masters tournament at Augusta, the previous winners, in their traditional green blazers, assemble for a dinner. Snead regularly enters the dining-room with a gymnastic kick to the top of the door-frame.

When he made his entrance in 1977, 'Slammin' Sammy' this time came up short. He groaned, 'I'm just getting too old'. A year earlier, Snead had had no trouble reaching the top, so at least two of the green jacket brigade, Gary Player and Arnold Palmer, were confused.

'I'll bet you $100 he was faking and can still do it', said Palmer to Player. 'You're on', said Gary. After dinner, Snead settled the bet — and Palmer pocketed a crisp $100 bill.

The name of Willie Park Jun. looms large in golf's ancient history. Born at Musselburgh, he played many famous matches and was not only a famous player in the late nineteenth and early twentieth centuries but, afterwards, won fame as a course designer.

He also designed a special club, 'Park's Patent Lofter', in which a very concave blade could send the ball high into the

'... and I got this one from a Greg Norman slice at the 15th.'

air with considerable backspin so that it would fall without any roll.

But he earned most fame as a putter and he won much of his great reputation with a favourite putter which he called 'Old Pawky'. The putter now hangs in the clubhouse of the Woking Club, Surrey, and round the shaft is a silver band containing Park's own words, 'It holed many a guid putt'.

In the early days of ladies' golf, voluminous skirts often made it difficult for their wearers to see the ball on the ground, particularly in a wind. Miss Eleanor Helme, writing in *After the Ball* (1931) recounted:

'So Miss Higgins of the U.S.A. earned immortal fame and the undying gratitude of her generation by inventing a piece of elastic which could be slipped from the waist (yes, we did have waists even if we had no ankles) downwards, so as to hold the irrepressible skirt in place.'

This piece of elastic became known as 'Miss Higgins'.

Any golfer worth his salt will tell you that a warm golf ball will travel further than a cold one. Some are so obsessed with the theory that they use two balls at alternate holes, keeping one warm in a trouser pocket.

The authors of *The Search for the Perfect Swing* conducted a study through the Golf Society of Great Britain Scientific Study and came up with this finding:

'A ball's coefficient of restitution — the liveliness, that is, with which it springs away again after being flattened against the clubface — is directly affected by its temperature; and keeping it warm can make it start off quite a bit faster from impact and thus fly quite a bit further from the tee. A drive which will carry 200 yards with the ball at 70°F (21°C) will carry only 185 yards when the ball is at freezing point.

'The effect upon a ball's temperature of keeping it in your

trouser pocket for minutes on a cold day, though, is very much less than the optimist may believe. Rubber is a poor conductor of heat, and it may take several hours for a ball to heat up all the way through, however warm it feels on its surface. But it loses heat only very slowly too; and it will thus have quite an effect on the length of a player's drive on a cold day for him to store a few balls in the boiler-house the night before, and then to use a different one every three or four holes, keeping the others in his trouser pockets.'

Golf's deadly ailment is the dreaded socket. It means hitting the ball on the socket or shank, where the shaft joins the clubhead, sending it off at an acute angle. Chamber's Dictionary simply describes it as 'a stroke with the socket of a golf club', and 'an act of shanking a golf ball'.

Golfers talk in hushed tones about the dreaded socket that can send their ball spearing away at right angles to their target. Professionals throw their hands up and walk away from anxious pupils trying to overcome the sockets, fearing it could infiltrate their own game. In rhyming slang the socket was known as a 'Lucy Locket' but more recently a 'Davy Crockett'.

Colourful Lee Trevino was at his best after a scorching round of 67 in the British Open at Muirfield.

He told interviewers, 'Normally, I say a hungry dog hunts better. But this morning I had a good breakfast. On a full stomach, butterflies do not have room to fly.'

Robert T. Jones, in his reminiscences, recounts the story of a wealthy American and his brush with an abrasive Scottish caddie:

'Back in the days when all Americans were both notoriously

rich and for the most part bad golfers', wrote Jones, 'one of our countrymen is supposed to have visited St Andrews, the cradle of the game, and played the Old Course. He had assigned to him one of the picturesque old caddies, so commonly encountered there, who know the game from beginning to end and are quite impatient of any trifling with it.

'Our friend played very badly and, as the round progressed, the relationship between him and his caddie became more and more strained. Finally, with great relief he put his ball into the hole on the home green and, thinking to recapture some of his caddie's esteem, he handed the old boy a tip of a gold sovereign, remarking as light-heartedly as he could, "Well, caddie, golf is a funny game, isn't it?"

"Aye", responded the old Scot, eyeing the gold coin and wagging his head ruefully, "but it was nae meant to be" '.

One of the earliest to proclaim the virtues of the game of golf was the novelist Tobias Smollett. In his book, *The Expedition of Humphrey Clinker*, he enthused:

'Hard by, in the fields called the Links, the citizens of Edinburgh divert themselves at a game called Golf, in which they use a curious kind of bat tipped with horn, and small elastic balls of leather, stuffed with feathers, rather less than tennis balls, but of a much harder consistency.

'These they strike with such force and dexterity from one hole to another, that they will fly to an incredible distance. Of this diversion the Scots are so fond that, when the weather will permit, you may see a multitude of all ranks, from the senator of justice to the lowest tradesman, mingled together, in their shirts, and following the balls with the utmost eagerness.

'Among others, I was shown one particular set of golfers, the youngest of whom was turned of four-score. They were all gentlemen of independent fortunes, who had amused themselves with this pastime for the best part of a century without having ever felt the least alarm from sickness or

36

disgust; and they never went to bed without having each the best part of a gallon of claret in his belly. Such uninterrupted exercise, co-operating with the keen air from the sea, must, without all doubt, keep the appetite always on edge, and steel the constitution against all the common attacks of distemper.'

The American *Golf Digest*, a magazine that has hit the one million mark in monthly sales, provided this golfing glossary:

GIMME: An uneasy agreement between players who cannot putt.

BALL: A dimpled sphere unsuited for anything except getting lost.

HANDICAP: A chronic limp, myopia, linquinal hernia. Also something which golfers lie about to their own detriment. Like a 20-handicapper saying, 'I shot to a nine'.

HOLE: A 4¼-inch excavation placed 400 yards from where a golfer, armed with an awkward weapon, will try to find it in four shots.

TRAP: Huge area of sand. It is also what the golfer opens when he finds his ball in a footprint. A hacker requires two strokes to get out, the second of which is cerebral.

ROUGH: Where the ball is kicked when nobody is looking. Also where the ball is hiding when everybody is looking. Nobody helps a hacker look for a ball unless they are sure he's in trouble.

CLUBS: Concealed weapons. A stick with the handle at the wrong end. An object which the golfer embraces with both hands no matter how many times it betrays him.

LIE: Where the ball reposes after being adjusted by a foot. Also the number uttered by a player after he holes out.

GOOD MISS: A solid whack which shears off every third blade of grass.

LIP: A place for growing a moustache. The overhanging edge of a bunker. The place where a great putt dies. What you get from your golfing buddy.

SHANK: What is left of Sunday's ham on Monday. An unconscious trick shot which courts cardiac arrest.

HOLE HIGH: Good shot, wrong direction. Often the result of larcenous feet.

HEAD: Something which the golfer and the criminal hold in a downward position. Something which neither uses. A thing which emits horrendous cries.

TEE: A tiny wooden stick which holds a ball above grass. The safest place for a frightened insect when a duffer swings.

PRO: The only doctor who will not tell you that your game is terminally ill.

BALL RETRIEVER: The 15th, and most important club in the bag.

BLAST: A shot from a bunker. Also a British expletive as a result of the result.

SLICE: The addiction of half the golfers who want to hit a straight ball.

HOOK: The addiction of the other half.

STARTING TIME: The last moment when golfers are seen laughing and joking.

LOCKER ROOM: A sanctuary for ugly nudists.

We have spoken earlier about Titanic Thompson, the sensationally good left-hander and hustler supreme. In truth, he didn't have the 'underworld' field to himself. Around about 1937, the critics were lauding the prowess of John Montague of Los Angeles. The most proficient player in the world, one conceded.

The *New Yorker Magazine* duly came out with this reference: 'Undoubtedly, the strangest golf story of the year was about John Montague of Los Angeles who, after being recognized by Grantland Rice and other golf authorities as the most proficient player in the world, was recognized by the authorities of New York State as a suspect in a hold-up.

'The Montague epic — his mysterious appearance in

'... and at the 3rd, did you not improve your lie in the bunker?'

California, his famous match against Bing Crosby, his ability to throw cards at the crack of a door, or when displeased, to hang his golfing competitors on the coat-racks in their lockers — has been too thoroughly recited in the Press for comment here.

'The whole affair, including Montague's shyness, which, now so explicable, was instantly and universally accepted, like Greta Garbo's, as the hallmark of a rich personality, belonging to the true Hollywood tradition.

'Golf seems to have a special fascination for characters whose careers belong to a world quite different from that of country clubs. None of them has achieved Montague's inconvenient excellence but several have been notable at least for their eccentricity.

'Al Capone was not a particularly able golfer, but he played honestly and with enjoyment. The same compliment cannot be paid to the late Leo Flynn, who was a member of Jack Dempsey's board of strategy when Dempsey was the world's heavyweight champion.

'Amiable and engaging off the golf-course, Flynn, who took up the game late in life and became a fanatical devotee, was irascible when playing, and though his scores were in the low 70s, he never had enough confidence in his ability to dispense with artificial aids.

'The most effective of these was a Negro caddie whom Flynn once hired by the month in Florida. Friends noticed that the caddie always walked barefoot. It was his duty, when Flynn's ball went in the rough, to pick it up with his unusually long toes and, without stooping down, deposit it quietly on the fairway.'

Walter Hagen, debonair, playboy champion of the 1930s, says his secret was never to hurry. Critics wrote that he had no regard for time — frequently he arrived at the tee straight from an all-night party — but he defended himself saying he respected time and tried to make the most of it. There was just as much in saving time as in spending it properly. It fitted the old Army gag about 'Hurry up and wait'. He didn't hurry, therefore he wasn't bothered with waiting.

He took up the story in his autobiography, 'From the minute I rose in the morning, I kept on an even keel until I reached the first tee. I got up in plenty of time to dress and breakfast leisurely and to arrive at the golf course just when I was due to play. There's a certain sort of rhythm in such a smoothed out routine that carried over to my game ... a rhythm that helped me avoid the jerky, gear-shifting movements which characterized the game of many easily upset or nervous golfers.

'There were a few times when I stepped up to tee off with not even one hour of sleep. One such occasion has been narrated incorrectly so often that I'm going to set it straight ...

'This particular exhibition match was scheduled for New Year's Day, at ten in the morning. My wife and I had been on a round-robin party on New Year's Eve and had ended up at a home a good half-hour drive from the club. My chauffeur came in and reminded me of the exhibition match.

'The sun had been up so long I'd no idea of the correct time. Checking my watch I found I had slightly less than thirty minutes to motor across to Pasadena. I arrived at the first tee wearing my dinner clothes and patent leather pumps. The few hundred people in the gallery thought that was great fun.

'I was sliding in all directions trying to tee off in those slippery-soled shoes and after several attempts I got my drive away. I gave the gallery the impression that I intended playing the entire match in those clothes.

'Then, after taking my second shot, I made my excuses and explained that I'd go into the clubhouse and dress for the game. Looking over the gallery I remarked that I thought a number of them hadn't been up too long, either. They laughed and agreed I had a lot of company.

'In the clubhouse I changed to regular golf clothes and

'A '72', that's wonderful. When are you going to play the other nine?'

spiked shoes. Even then, for the next several holes, I noticed that the fairway was much more slippery than it had ever seemed the dozens of times I'd played it. I managed to keep my footing and balance and went on to win my match with a 68.'

A cute insight into early life at the Metropolitan Club, Melbourne, appears in the club records. Members' response to a suggestion-box included:

That a plank bridge be placed across the water at Dog Island and that nets and poles be provided (golf balls floated in those days).

Where one is forced to drink tea let that tea be good.

That the whiskies be either increased from three-quarter ones, or the measuring be left to the discretion of members.

Boys and men should be prohibited from bathing in the water hole off the ninth fairway in a nude state, especially as ladies use the links.

That cows should not be tethered in the centre of a fairway in playing hours.

Supplies of black-beaded pins and hair pins be available in the ladies dressing room, also that clocks be kept at the correct hour so that members might catch their trains.

The colourful history of the Royal Hong Kong Club at Fanling, so close to the border of China, is chockful of delightful anecdotes.

None better than an item from the year 1922 which reports that a picture gallery was erected near the clubhouse entrance and members became curious about a picture of a padre attempting to hit a ball with half a dozen broken clubs lying nearby and a puzzled expression on his face.

Such was the speculation over the Reverend gentleman's exclamation that members conducted a contest, 'What the

Padre said' and asked the donor to be the judge. The donor removed the picture.

Henry Longhurst set out to achieve two things in his back-page golf column that adorned the London *Sunday Times* for twenty years. Firstly, it had to contain one funny anecdote for retelling later that morning at the clubhouse bar and second, the column needed to be short enough to be read 'during five minutes in the loo'.

The sports world mourned the passing of Henry Longhurst. His dry wit and fruity voice over television and sports column raised countless chuckles. The man who penned so many of his columns from his home in a windmill is credited with lifting 'a quite ridiculous game to sublime heights'. He called golf the supreme 'do it yourself' game, the Esperanto of Sport, the game of a lifetime — from eight to eighty.

Alistair Cook, writing a foreword to a book containing an edited version of Longhurst's works, began, 'He is recognizable in the first few sentences as a sly, wry, rheumy-eyed observer of human beings who happened to choose golf to illustrate their fusses and follies'.

Such was his influence in the golf world that, in the far-distant Antipodes, the Royal Sydney Club lowered its flag to half-mast to salute his passing.

Three quotations that reflect his impish humour:

On putting: 'The art of putting at golf resembles that of goalkeeper at soccer, in being a game within a game. Furthermore, as I remember so often reflecting as I leant nonchalantly against the uprights — having played in goal since the age of eight — both are games which enable a fellow with a certain crafty cunning to neutralize the efforts of stronger, braver men, and this in any walk of life is a source of much inward satisfaction.'

On practice: 'I take the revolutionary view that all this talk

44

about the virtues of practice, for the average club golfer at any rate, is a snare and a delusion.'

On temper: 'To me at any rate, the most exquisitely satisfying act in the world of golf is that of throwing a club.'

A zonk on the head cemented a fast friendship between golfer Doug Sanders and the United States Vice President Agnew.

The Vice President, although a mediocre player, has been much sought after as a personality for pro-amateur events. It was at the Bob Hope Classic that Agnew creased Sanders' head with a wayward shot.

The Vice President, in thanking Sanders for the painful memory of the day's golf, sent the professional a memento in the form of a silver tray, suitably engraved, including, in large letters, the word FORE.

'I asked my caddie for a sand wedge and he came back ten minutes later with a ham on rye.' (Chi Chi Rodriguez.)

'My caddie and I should have bought tickets we were outside the ropes so often.' (Dave Hill).

Such are the day by day quips among the professionals about that downtrodden race, the caddies. The first caddies, of course, were dour Scots and their successors can be seen today, dressed in raggle-taggle clothing and cloth caps to ward off the chill winds of the Atlantic and the Irish Sea, and humping golf bags across the swills and burns.

Peter Dobereiner once wrote: 'It is the physical condition of the rank and file which most strongly suggests combat and deprivation. Fresh wounds, old bruises turning parchment coloured at the edges, and bleary eyes picked out in vivid shades of crimson heighten the fantasy. These are the men, however, who day after day hump bags of clubs too heavy for most mortals to transport further than from car boot to trolley, for distances up to ten miles. Although they look to be in the extremes of mortal disintegration they nevertheless perform feats of endurance which would shame the general run of spade-leaning navvies.'

So much for the old British caddies. Their American counterparts are all but non-existent due, of course, to automatons in the shape of sleek electric carts which hustle golfers from shot to shot.

On tour there is a small but regular bunch of these gypsies of the fairways. They've got names such as Wolfman and Primo and Golf Ball and Blackie and the Baron. They are for ever on the lookout for a 'good bag', which simply means a successful pro. Who is a 'good bag' then?

Angelo Argea, the celebrated long-time caddie for Jack Nicklaus, in his book *The Bear and I*, says 'good' doesn't necessarily mean pros who consistently earn fat cheques. Some of the biggest winners have combination locks on their wallets. So there are obviously other factors involved. Generosity, sensitivity, a little compassion, and even temper and a ton of ability — those are the qualities that make up a 'good bag'. The silver-haired Angelo concedes that with Jack Nicklaus he's got a 'great bag'.

Angelo caddies in style. Frequently he flies in Nicklaus's private plane, his duties for the superstar embrace valet work and he is welcomed, as a personality, into famous homes.

But for the most part of a tour caddies are a battling lot of nomadic carriers who are forced to pitch tents, curl up on lawns or sleep eight to a room in a frowsy motel 'where gnats are buzzing around the green lights over the doors and cigarette burns are on everything from the carpeting to the Gideon Bible'.

Angelo relates the strange story of one of them. 'This caddie tore the backseat out of his Volkswagen and set up housekeeping there — he slept, ate, did his laundry, read the comics, bathed, listened to his transistor radio, entertained lady friends and did everything but raise a family in those close

46

'Damn it, Smith, this is the only way I can reach the 7th in 2.'

quarters as he moved from tournament to tournament, searching for a good bag.

'His sleep was often interrupted by the local constable shining a flashlight in his face and telling him to get out of town by sunrise or sooner. So one night he decided it would be a safer bet if he parked on the seashore, where his car would be mistaken as a temporary haven for lovers and where the sound of the waves would lull him into deep slumber. He drove his vehicle out to a secluded, cove-like area just a few inches from the water line, dined on a can of pork and beans, set his alarm clock, and drifted into dreamland.

'Around 5 a.m. he was awakened by a gurgling noise. He rubbed his eyes and looked outside, but all he could see was water—it was as if he were gazing into an aquarium through each window. Seaweed and tiny fish and shells were floating all around and for a moment he thought he had died in his sleep and been reincarnated as Jacques Cousteau. A few more inches and his VW could have been a submarine. It had rained heavily during the night and the tide had risen.

'Just as he was about to grin and bear his watery grave, he felt a pulling motion and heard muffled voices. He was being dredged out by a local rescue unit.'

Angelo tells us that the caddie didn't go to work that day at the golf course, or the next day. In fact, he hasn't been seen on tour since.

Tim Evans is a script writer for the popular Don Lane television show and he's a judge for the *New Faces* programme. More importantly, he happens to be the funniest man in Australian golf, a modest middle-mark performer guaranteed to create high merriment among any fourball group.

Playing in a national PGA pro-amateur at Royal Melbourne, he watched sympathetically as the husky New Zealander, John Lister, swatted angrily at a host of marauding, sticky flies. 'You know', said Tim, 'I've always wondered why Noah didn't kill both of them when he had the chance'.

Tim offered his own contribution to the spate of Irish jokes that were in popular circulation. At a time when DC10 aircraft were grounded all around the world following several disasters, he volunteered the news that the Irish airlines were sympathetic though they didn't own any DC10s. So they had grounded two DC3s and a DC4.

And then there was this fellow who went out for his first game of golf. He did all the things a learner is supposed to do ... kept his head down ... kept his eye firmly on the ball. Somebody stole his buggy.

Tim Evans recounts the contest between two 30-handicappers for the club's wooden spoon. When it was all over, the loser slumped disconsolately at the end of the bar. A mate moved across and inquired how he'd fared.

'You wouldn't believe it', the loser responded. 'I was three up with four holes to play, then he gets hot and throws four straight fifteens at me.'

Sydney *Sun* golf critic, Terry Smith, tells the story of left-hander, Len Nettlefold, who ruled Tasmanian golf for some twenty years. Nettlefold's amateur titles included two Australian crowns and eight successes in the Tasmanian championship.

Smith recounts: 'The name Nettlefold became a household word in Tasmania when Len and his father built up a million-dollar business selling farm machinery and cars. His dad, Robert Nettlefold, is said to have begun the business with thirty shillings in his pocket and a bicycle and a hat for his office. When Len was six holes down to George Forsett with just seven holes to play in the 1926 Australian title final at Royal Adelaide, Nettlefold Sen. said, "Son, get out of this and you can have my Buick". Young Nettlefold left the clubhouse in the Buick.'

'Oh look, he's fetched it for you.'

Australian professional, Bruce Crampton, who earned fame and fortune in a long stint on the American circuit, also won a reputation for grim, humourless and unrelenting play. The stony-faced Sydney practitioner from time to time bridled at the barbs concerning his icy on-course disposition.

Crampton countered sharply, 'You don't see the captain of a 747 jet making jokes when he's coming in to land, do you? The golf course is my office, where I work. If the people want to be entertained they should go to see a good show. If they want to see good golf shots, that's something else. That's all I'm able to do. If I were an actor I'd be in Hollywood.'

But we can reveal that Crampton owned a little toy monkey which he says resembled a professional golfer. When a fifteen-foot putt for a birdie rolled in, it clanged the cymbals in its mitts repeatedly. And for a missed four-foot par putt, the monkey screeched and its eyes bugged out.

With an ugly, stooping, ducking shoulder motion, Jim Ferrier wasn't a golfer to delight the purists. But he was a king on the Australian amateur scene until he took off to the United States to embark on a professional career that was subsequently highlighted by his victory in the 1947 American PGA championship. The secret of his success was a lethal short game and an equally deadly putting stroke. He was a ruthless opponent. Rivals nicknamed him the 'Undertaker'. They said he not only beat his opponents; he buried them as well.

The professional field for the 1969 Australian Open was up in arms because of Royal Sydney Club's alleged stuffy attitude in restricting admission to outsiders, including players' wives.

Lee Trevino, coming up the final fairway, turned to the big gallery on his heels and said, 'The only way I can get into that clubhouse is if I overhit this next shot and the ball finishes up in that verandah lounge'.

Trevino's humour is unmatched on and off the golf course. Some of his critics claim it is a sharp form of gamesmanship. Other players say they enjoy his company and his good humour helps to relax them.

Trevino summed up his own sunny philosophy this way, 'I'm just like a duck. I wake up to a new world every day.'

Male domination of the golf scene finally got under the skin of a small army of dedicated Brisbane female players. These 'associates' joined forces and in 1969 opened the first Australian woman-controlled club, the McLeod Country Club, named after Miss Gertrude McLeod, a president of the Australian Ladies Golf Union and a notable Queensland administrator. By 1975 they had built a $200,000 clubhouse and though male players were subsequently admitted, they were refused voting powers. The original dollar bill which purchased the freehold title to 123 acres of prime land at Mt Ommaney in 1968 is still on display inside the clubhouse.

Three versions of the most crucial word in golf: pressure.

FRANK BEARD: 'You've probably watched a pro miss a simple putt on television and wondered how it could happen. The point is that it's the pressure that makes a situation difficult. There are golfers who can make a thousand straight eighteen-inch putts if no money is at stake, or if you're talking five bucks a putt. But raise the ante and they couldn't hit the hole.

'What's the choking point? A hundred dollars? A thousand? A million? Your life? What would you bet?'

LEE TREVINO: 'When you are playing for five bucks and you've got two bucks in your pocket—that's pressure. Where's the pressure when you've got a five-footer for the Open? Hole it or miss it, you still wind up with a pocket full of dollars.'

GEORGE ARCHER: 'Real pressure is when, as a kid, you're putting under street lights for a lot of dough and all you've got in your pocket is a dime for a ball marker.'

Professional Gene Littler confessed to mixed emotions about being labelled 'Gene the Machine'. He said, 'I know it's intended as a compliment, but a machine I'm not. I read that and I get a little disturbed when I'm playing bad. I'm complimented in a way but the term seems a trifle ridiculous when I'm trying to hit a ball from out of the bushes.'

Surely the most remarkable round of golf ever played belonged to an American, Joe Ezar, and the card, dated 1936, is still on display in an Italian golf club.

It all happpened during the Italian Open played out on the picturesque Sestieres Golf Club. Ezar fired a winning last round 64, but it wasn't so much the sizzling low score as the way it was achieved that was so incredible.

After playing the third round of the tournament, Ezar gave a skilful display of trick shots on the practice putting-green. The club president made Ezar a presentation and added that if the American could nominate his shots with such precision then he could well break the course record of 67 on the final day. The president offered him a 1,000 lire incentive.

'How much for a 64?' Ezar inquired. The president told him a cheque for 4,000 lire would be his if he could shoot 64 in the final round.

Ezar casually asked the president for his cigarette pack and, watched by the big crowd, wrote down his card for a score of 64. It seemed a light-hearted gesture. But tension mounted next day when the fans saw Ezar start out matching hole-by-hole the predicted round.

The American met a major hurdle at the par-five 9th on which he had predicted the previous evening he would register an eagle three. His second shot finished fifty yards short of the green and the dream of his perfect round seemed doomed. But he executed the most perfect chip shot and the ball disappeared into the cup for the nominated eagle three.

Ezar completed the back nine exactly as he predicted. The president wrote out a 4,000 lire cheque on the spot. Experts rated Ezar's round a 100,000 odds gamble.

Ezar made one trip to Australia. He arrived without any clubs and had to borrow a set.

The mighty Argentinian golfer, Roberto de Vicenzo, looked to have the Wills Masters neatly parcelled up at Kensington, NSW. Suddenly, on the back nine, he began to falter.

Alan Murray, his nearest rival but a long way behind, watched it all on the television screen. The de Vicenzo collapse continued until an official came up to Murray in the clubhouse and said, 'You'd better shoe up, there's going to be a play-off'.

Murray confessed afterwards he was in a complete daze. He had drunk seven brandies, one for every faltering bogey de Vicenzo had taken on the homeward run! But he went back out on the course and beat the Argentinian on the first play-off hole.

'After that, I'm giving up drinking carrot juice', observed one professional in the gallery.

During the blackest moments of World War II a remarkable story emerged.

The scene was the Stalag Luft 3 prison camp for RAF air-crew officers. A hickory-shafted lady's mashie had turned up in the camp and its discovery had caused great excitement. Nobody knew, or cared, how such an unlikely implement came to be in a POW camp in the middle of the forest of Sagan.

Peter Dobereiner unfolds the story: 'Immediately, the history of the golf ball was re-enacted in miniature. The prisoners' first ball was made by winding string around a wooden core and covering it with cloth. Then someone found

'But I promise, Harold, I won't make you late for tee-off.'

some shreds of rubber and, just like Sandy Herd with the coming of the Haskett rubber-core ball, he spread-eagled the field with his jerry-built missile. Some tried to remain faithful to their string gutties but progress would not be denied.

'The rubber-bound ball, covered with medical sticking plaster, had come to stay. The technique was further refined by cutting up rubber-soled shoes and producing leather-covered balls which conformed exactly to the specifications of the Royal and Ancient Golf Club: 1.62 inches in diameter and 1.62 ounces in weight.

'As the golf craze grew, the prisoners turned their attention to clubmaking. Shafts were whittled by penknife and heads cast from melted stovepipes in moulds made of soap. The course evolved gradually, again following the pattern of the original medieval process, with the first games being played haphazardly between the huts. In time, as the homemade equipment proliferated and more prisoners began to play, the course became formalized, nine holes with 'browns' of packed sand, bunkers, and contoured approaches. Eventually, parcels from home brought real clubs and proper balls, and golf at Stalag Luft 3 caught up with the twentieth century. Tuition was organized for learners, exhibitions were arranged by hot-shot players, and a championship was held.

'The severest penalty in the history of golf faced the man who played a loose shot. Anyone stepping over the rail which marked the inner perimeter was likely to be shot by the guards. In time the Germans came to adopt an attitude of uneasy tolerance and a white coat was issued to be worn as a mark of good faith that the wearer was simply retrieving a golf ball and not trying to escape.

'It was ironic that the Germans should have watched these harmless golfing activities with such mistrust. For under their noses one of the most daring escapes of the War was being engineered, via a tunnel dug under cover of a wooden vaulting horse. The Germans barely gave the vaulters a second look.'

For years and years, professional golfers were nothing more than lackies and were forced to use the servants' entrance to golf clubs.

Walter Hagen, the dandy who always travelled first class, changed all that. On his first English tour, he checked into the Ritz in London with his secretary and he dazzled reporters with the splendour of his living.

A few clubs, on his British tour, wouldn't allow him into their dining rooms. He responded by parking in front of these offending institutions in a Rolls Royce, where he had an elaborate picnic lunch served to him.

The 'needle' can cost you strokes, and friends, too, says Gene O'Brien of the slick little American *Golf World* magazine. Gamesmanship? You be the judge.

Says O'Brien: 'The power of suggestion is usually caused by known, or unknown, acts of "needling". The art of needling is practised by some golfers to gain advantage over their opponents.

'The few times I tried to use the needle it usually backfired because my opponents had their hearing aids turned off. I had a most proficient needler at my club and it's a wonder he is still alive. All he would have to do is mention the fact that a little slice would land his competitor's ball in the water and in many cases the suggestion drew the ball into the water. I do not recommend the needle because I think it's a bit on the seamy side of good sportsmanship.

'Friendly jesting is not to be confused with the sharp and sometimes large needle. To the average high handicapper the needle in most cases has just the opposite effect. I showed a very adept needler how to cut ten strokes off his game just by learning to keep his mouth shut.

'The most deadly of the needlers happen to be women. They are also charming and tactful at the art. One lady I remember did everything but bring her doctors and an ambu-

'Do I take it that you'll be finding another partner for the next Pro-Am?'

lance to the course. She was the most unhealthy 5-handi-capper alive. She had diseases that hadn't been discovered yet and employed the sympathy needle to great advantage, except to those who got used to wearing ear-plugs.

'Then you had the usual associate who in teeing off in a club tournament would explain why she should never be on the course with all her problems of taking care of her children, housework, etc. The more common one is, "I ought to just give you the match now, it's silly of me to think I can beat you".

'I was starting some mixed groups one day and this guy's wife was talking up a storm. One of the men was getting ready to hit his tee shot and the fellow who owned the talking machine said, "Don't you know good golf etiquette, trying to hit your ball while my wife is talking?" His wife stopped for about thirty seconds.

'It is well known that some forms of conversation can cost you strokes. It's also as well to be able to learn to play your own game and black out the powers of suggestion. If the conversation of your companions ruins your concentration you have to figure some way to block it out. I don't see how you can get over the ball and be thinking about stocks and bonds, lemon pie, riots, politics, birth control and sex.'

Jimmy Demaret, famous for his peacock hues on the course, came out wearing a pair of chartreuse slacks, an orange shirt and checkered tam. As he stood on the tee he felt a hand strok-ing his trousers. He looked around, in a hurry, and there was a woman who had broken 60 some years ago and with no trouble

'Young man', she said, 'do you mind if I feel your trousers?'

Demaret nodded in a confused, embarrassed way. When she had finished she turned around and screamed at the top of her scratchy voice, 'It's charmeuse, Mabel. Just as I said!'

Heather, along with firewater and a peculiar stuff called haggis that they wrap up stomach in some unfortunate sheep's stomach, is famed as a product of Scotland and it spells doom to the golfer. It's mighty tough going ploughing through the stuff.

British golfer Clive Clark says that of course the great secret of getting out of heather is ... well, to get out. There is no secret. Over-ambitious golfers have found themselves still ensnared four shots later.

A good friend of Clive Clark, whose nickname is Cutty (he slices everything) decided that the best approach would be to have a specially prepared club. He ground his wedge until the leading edge resembled a razor blade.

Clark witnessed his first shot with the club. It occurred on the 17th hole during a tense moment in the Sunday afternoon fourball. Cutty gave the shot his all. Heather sprayed in all directions, and heads turned skywards. But after ten seconds it was clear that no golf ball was up there. Cutty inspected the trench that he had gouged, but there was no evidence there of the whereabouts of his golf ball.

Then it was spotted, firmly attached to the leading edge of his new toy! It's a true story.

Golf World asked Sam Snead his favourite golf story.

Old Sam beamed and related: 'Well, this actually happened. I was over in York, England. There was this man and his wife. She didn't know how to play golf. She didn't play. And of course, he played a little golf. And they went out to the tournament we were playing in York.

'This professional came up the 18th and he sliced his ball over to the right of the green into the trash. And he hit the ball from the trash into the trap. And from the trap he got it out into the high grass short of the green. So this guy watching says, "Gee, he's having a terrible day".

'From there, the player put it in the hole. And she said, "Well now he's got a real problem".'

How those stories about the one and only Walter Hagen have enriched golf humour.

At the Piccadilly World Match Play championship, Hagen's British caddie, Walter Smith, then eighty-two years of age, reminisced about his famous master. After completing sixteen years' Army service, Smith had met Hagen at Addington Golf Club, near London. Hagen had observed, 'Damn it, you've got a good swing. Will you work for me?'

Smithy gleefully accepted and served both as caddie and valet to Hagen not only in Britain but in places such as Calcutta, Bali, Japan, Hawaii and California.

'Wherever we went, we never hurried', recalled Smithy. 'One morning there was a bit of a panic to get off a sleeping-car in Glasgow, but that didn't bother Walter. He had a porter pushing his breakfast along the platform on a trolley, and he walked along eating it.'

Hagen, avowed Smithy, never swore. The most he might do was say 'God damn. I wish I had that baby over again.'

But the maestro was an inveterate poacher. One day, shooting grouse from a coasting Lincoln Zephyr somewhere in New Galloway, they were caught by the owner of the estate. Then the Hagen charm was brought into play, and master and valet-cum-caddie ended up drinking Scotch in the ancestral castle.

A good payer? 'The most generous man you ever met', said Smithy.'You know, I am still being paid by his family, even now.'

Believe it or not, in America there is a golf course with a billabong. You'll find it at Torrey Pines, the scene of the San Diego Open in 1975 when Australia's Bruce Devlin found the water on the final hole. Devlin resolved to slosh the ball out of the pond. Six strokes later...! Officials decided to erect a plaque, calling it 'Devlin's Pond' but Bruce suggested Australianizing the name to billabong. He thought it a neat idea even though the pond had cost him $3,000 and an ugly 10 on his card.

Unknown in Australian golf but apparently in vogue overseas is the intimidating business of 'Woofs'.

Webster Evans, in his *Encyclopaedia of Golf,* describes 'Woofs' thus: 'A variation on the normal method of handicapping, in which the less good player is allowed "Woofs" instead of strokes. He is allowed to use his "Woofs"—by shouting "Woof" or pretending that he is about to do so—at any time during the game; the strain is on the better player because he never knows when a "Woof" is coming. "Woofs" are, of course, used only in light-hearted games; and are not often met with at all these days.'

Golfers superstitious? You'd better believe it.

I once watched Gary Player, all set for a big tournament round, take possession of a box of brand-new balls. He cast aside all the odd numbered balls and retained only the even numbered. In fact his lucky number is Two.

Jack Nicklaus asks his caddie to provide a shuttle service with new balls during a round. The Golden Bear uses six new balls a round and never the same one for two holes running. A simple reason, of course—his swing exerts a concussion force of half a ton and a hit ball takes ten minutes to regain its proper shape.

Severiano Ballesteros will not play with a Number Three ball because he says it psychs him into three-putting.

Australian star, Peter Thomson, five times winner of the British Open, constantly wears on his wrist a copper bracelet, the gift of a white hunter in Rhodesia. Previously, he had tried a Kenyan loop of elephant hair, Indian herbs and Chinese incantations in a bid to clear up an arthritic wrist.

During a Ryder Cup match at Muirfield, Scotland, Jack Nicklaus and Tom Weiskopf were teamed together for the United States against Britain. It seems that Weiskopf insists on having three dimes in his pocket during a round and he had showed up at tee time with only two.

Nicklaus turned to some officials and said, 'Can you imagine that? Tom's frantic because he lost one of his dimes and he always plays with three in his pocket.'

Then Nicklaus sheepishly confided, 'I'll tell you something. I always play with three pennies. And when I mark the ball, I always do it with tails up.'

And even caddies are superstitious. When Al Geiberger posted his historic round of 59, the caddie refused to follow orders to hand his professional a new ball every three holes. The caddie didn't want to put the hex on a ball that was doing a great job and Al used it for the entire round.

The year was 1966—Arnold Palmer's only successful tilt at the prestigious Australian Open crown.

Golf writer, Terry Smith, was the man on the spot in this delightful anecdote. It concerns Ted 'Cricket' Ball, a cavalier Sydney pro conspicuous by his lightning-fast swing, roguish humour and the inevitable cigarette dangling from his mouth.

Ball was drawn to play with Palmer and he introduced himself to the famous American on the first tee. Palmer shook hands dutifully but clearly had forgotten his playing partner's name moments later.

In a sensational start to the Open, Ted Ball fired birdie-birdie-birdie-par-eagle — five under the card in the first five holes!

Arnold Palmer, astonished by what he had witnessed, asked him on the next tee, 'What did you say your name was?'

Ball, quick as a flash, replied, 'Arnold Palmer'.

'I see Frisby's still having trouble with his putting.'

When Jerry Pate's ball during an American tournament hit a fairway sprinkler-head, it took a perverse bounce in the air and came down inside the front of the shirt of a gallery marshal. The official on the spot, a stickler for the rules, told the marshal not to make a move for the ball and to let the player retrieve it and identify it.

Nearby, a comely miss whose attributes were by no means hidden in her summer garb asked innocently, 'What if that happened to me?'

The official replied, 'Well, we would find some discreet way to get around the problem.'

She thought about it and sighed, 'I guess it would depend on the player'.

Andy Bean is a strapping young giant American professional, a tournament winner with a healthy reputation for strong-arm hitting. It didn't do his reputation any harm, either, the day he picked up an alligator and wrestled it.

At least that's the popular media version. 'Alligator Wrestler Takes Lead', trumpeted one sports page after Bean's victory at Doral. And when you consider, too, that Andy Bean had chewed up a golf ball, well, here was hot copy for the sports writers.

Eating-the-golf-ball act came after Bean's Florida University team had lost out to Wake Forest University. Bean was sitting behind the wheel of a station-wagon, waiting impatiently to drive a team-mate to the airport. He held up a golf ball for closer inspection — they said it looked like an aspirin in his huge hand — and he sank his teeth into the cover, leaving the ball looking like a friar's head. Bean handed the ball out the window and said, 'Here, take it. I've eaten my last golf ball. I'm going off the diet.'

Which brings us to the alligator business. He was playing in the pro qualifying school with Sandy Galbraith, who had never seen an alligator before.

Andy's version: 'I've been around alligators all my life; there were always three or four around the golf courses where I grew up. Anyway, we were playing the 16th hole when a 'gator came out of the lake to sun itself. It wasn't too big, maybe six, six and a half feet, and I said to Sandy, "What would you do if I went over and grabbed him?"'

'Well, Sandy went nuts, so I just walked over to that ol' 'gator and grabbed him by the tail. He was more scared of me than I was of him and he slid back into the water.

'A chap on the walkie-talkie put over that Bean had just picked up an alligator and thrown him into the lake. Since then it's gotten out of all proportion. People ask me about the time I picked up a 'gator, whipped him around over my head a couple of times and threw him out into the middle of the lake.'

Bean agrees the whole business has given him an identity — as a golf-ball-devouring, alligator-wrestling pro who can also hit a golfball out of sight. Oh yes, he also happens to be a tournament winner, too, six times over.

So you've battled the winds and the sleet and hacked out of blackboy bushes and clingy pigface and you reckon you've done it hard out on the golf course.

Well, you haven't played Elephant Hills course, near Victoria Falls on the border of what is now Zimbabwe, where they stage an annual professional classic tournament. Mortar shells fired by guerrillas from across the Zambezi River don't exactly make for a smooth backswing.

The wildlife isn't much help, either, which brings us to Britain's Noel Hunt and his most famous bogey.

Hunt was playing the 191-yard 8th hole and he'd hit into the edge of a pond only to discover a sleeping crocodile a few yards from the ball. Pluckily he removed his shoes and socks while his playing partner, Warren Humphreys, stood by as a bodyguard. Humphreys protected Hunt's rear with an eight-iron, which was probably not enough club.

Hunt then played 'the quickest wedge shot of my life', knocked the ball on the green and got down in two putts.

The portly South African, Bobby Locke, turned American golf upside-down when he arrived on their tournament scene and plundered the prize-money. The Yanks were stunned that this venerable looking gentleman who aimed thirty yards to the right to bend the ball back on to the fairway could upstage their champions.

Inducted to the Hall of Fame at Pinehurst years afterwards, Locke quipped, 'You know, when I first came to the States, I nearly lost four of the first six tournaments I played'. Then he told his audience that he wasn't so much a golfer as he was a singer!

Sam Snead had once chided him, 'You're gripping too weakly with your left hand'. Locke promptly countered, 'I accept my cheques with my right hand'.

Japan is the most golf-nutty country in the world. There are an estimated thirty million golf devotees, though the bulk of them never ever get to hit a ball on one of the country's congested courses. For them, golf action is confined to driving ranges. There are some 500 commercial ranges, but countless more tiny nets erected on the myriad flat-top roofs you see when driving in to Tokyo.

Land, of course, is so precious in Japan, that the country can't afford the extravagance of turning large tracts over to golf. And those courses that exist are many long miles from the city limits.

So the driving range is a way of life. At times long queues form at the giant Shiba Park range, a triple-storied construction that accommodates 20,000 players a week. Balls fly out from the bays like a stream of confetti.

We heard of one young Japanese professional, Tsuneyuki

Nakajima, who rigged up a makeshift range in his back yard where he hit 1,500 balls a day. To make the whole exercise more realistic he had set up an outdoor 'shower' so he could practise his shots in the rain, and also a large fan which provided windy conditions. Finally, in his garden he had a practice bunker, and in the bunker were five kinds of sand!

Sam Snead reckons every golf instructor has had at least one student he wished had never put on spikes. For him it was a man who actually flew his divots farther than he did the ball.

Recounted Sam: 'This man came to me for a lesson and started hitting some shots with the fastest, jerkiest, least rhythmical swing I'd ever seen. He had sods flying so fast and furious I felt like I was in the middle of World War II.

'After a few minutes this human plough was gasping and panting, and making my lesson tee look like sowing time in the Corn Belt. Somehow I had to stop this mutilation. I had to come up with something that would slow him down and put a little rhythm into his stroke.

"You know", I finally said, "a lot of the old-time players used to swing in waltz time — tra-la-la-la *BOOM* tra-la, tra-la; tra-la-la-la *BOOM* tra-la, tra-la ..."

'My man looked at me and smiled.

"I should know something about that", he said, "I'm a professional dancer".

'I told him to stop jitterbugging and start waltzing. He did, and I've never seen anyone improve so much, so fast, in my whole life. In just seconds he went from idiot to scholar, from zero right up the ladder.'

Toukley (New South Wales) professional, Tom Linskey, organized a party of twenty-four Australian golfers on an excursion of British golf courses, including the famous Open courses.

The Australians showed great interest in Britain's beautiful greens and lawns. Visiting one stately home near the

Turnberry Club, Perc Edwards of The Lakes, Sydney, quizzed the gardener, 'Just how can you produce such magnificent lawns?'

The gardener shrugged his shoulders and said, 'You just water them, fertilize them and mow them for 400 years'.

Sir Walter Simpson once described a golf links as, 'A place where rabbits and professionals earn a precarious living'.

No doubt about it, life was precarious for those early-day Scottish pros who had to be able to turn their hand to club-making, caddying and playing.

Horace Hutchinson took this beady look at them: 'One can divide into three classes those who derive a precarious subsistence from the game of golf: professional club-makers, professional players who eke out existence by work in the club-makers' shops and professional caddies who would be professional players if they played well enough ... The professional ... is a feckless, reckless creature ... He works at odd times, job work or time work, in the shops, but he only does it when reduced to an extremity. If he were ordinarily thrifty he would lay by in the autumn sufficient to carry him through the season of his discontent, when no golf is. He can lightly earn seven and sixpence a day by carrying clubs ... Many are engaged in a kind of body-service to their masters at £1 a week, which usually includes the advantage of a breakfast at their master's house and the disadvantage of having to black his boots. Occasionally they combine with golf-playing more general branches of industry which they pursue in a spasmodic fashion. Thus, when we asked one of them whether a brother professional had no other trade than that of golf, he replied, "Oh aye! He has that — he breaks stanes".'

Michael Parkinson, sports observer and television interviewer, these days is as well known in Australia as in his native

England. His passions are soccer and cricket and one of his pet dislikes is golf. So it was a case of putting the cat among the pigeons when the London *Sunday Times* once asked him to deputise for Henry Longhurst in the back page golf column.

This is how Parkinson tackled his assignment:

'While Mr Henry Longhurst takes that well-deserved rest from these columns can I be allowed a word in edgeways on the subject of golf? I might as well be frank and tell you from the start that I think golf is a bore, a drag, a 24-carat yawn. As a game to be played it comes bottom of my list somewhere between clay-pigeon shooting and underwater cyclo-cross and as a spectator sport it hardly registers. I would consider being assigned coverage of a golf match a punishment equalled only in its tedium to being asked to report a speech by Aviary Birdcage or being required to watch grass grow.

'I only express myself strongly because I feel it's time that someone spoke out against that ghastly legion of golfers who threaten to inherit the earth. It seems to me that every day friends whom I had once considered normal, intelligent human beings reveal themselves as golf fanatics unable to talk of anything beyond 'handicaps' and 'swings' and the like.

'Every car I ride in is cluttered with golfbags, everyone I work with spends two or three minutes each day practising iron shots on the office floor. You can tell by the glazed look in their eyes that reason has departed and all that remains is an insane fantasy about beating Gary Player or holing-in-one at Royal Birkdale. A few days ago I travelled in a lift sixteen floors with two friends who stood either side of me practising shots with imaginary irons and imaginary golf balls.

"Did you enjoy that?" I asked when we reached the ground floor.

"I think I played that hole quite well", said one.

"When next we travel in a lift can I caddie?" I asked in my most cynical manner. They looked one to the other in despair and I realized I was the odd man out.

'*You found which little white ball, where?*'

'Is there no one in Britain who shares my views on golf? Golf addicts would say not. Like anglers and lady wrestlers, they are adept at selling their sport. They are considerably helped in their task by the people who write about the game. It is a remarkable fact that the most tedious game in the world should inspire the talented pens of Bernard Darwin, Henry Longhurst, Stephen Potter, Peter Dobereiner to name but a few. Few sports, save cricket, have gained such loving and skilled attention from the people who write about them.

'They must be blessed with magic eyes for they don't see what I see. I like my sports to have colour, movement, physical as well as mental conflict. How can golf satisfy these needs? Which golfer ever made you gasp like George Best or Bobby Charlton or Sobers or Laver? Where is the beauty in the game, the spectacle? In the final analysis golf presents the identical picture of someone walking at a leisurely pace through the countryside stopping every now and again to flick a dandelion head with his walking-stick.

'For such a simple game it attracts a lot of claptrap. Anyone disputing what I say should delve into *The Search for the Perfect Swing*. The book was commissioned by the late Sir Aynsley Bridgland, who spent £60,000 on detailed scientific research into the secret of the golfer's ideal swing. The book is stuffed with the sort of information which golfers will lap up, but which I believe only goes to prove they're potty. The book tells us that a golfer is a fixed pivotal double lever two pendulum hub and anyone who plays the game could do well to remind himself of the fact every time he lines up for a shot.

'Other little known facts that every "fixed pivotal double lever two pendulum hub" should know are: during a drive the face of the club is in contact with the ball for only half a thousandth of a second which means that even the rabbit version of the "fixed pivotal double lever two pendulum hub" who plays maybe 100 shots a round, only spends one twentieth of a second hitting the ball. Which hardly seems worthwhile until you consider that FPDLTPH's like Arnold

Palmer who make up to £400,000 winning the U.S. Open are on a pay rate of £2 a second.

'What is more, all you golf addicts should keep your balls warm this winter. The book says that a 200-yard drive with the ball at 70ºF will be cut to 185 yards if the ball is at freezing point.

'I remain unmoved by all this. I leave the ooh's and aah's of such revelations to the like of Mr Longhurst who no doubt even now wherever he might be is putting his golf balls in a slow oven.'

The story is told that a typically English fourball had waited up to ten minutes on every shot behind a typically American fourball on one of the lush Bahamian courses. After they had taken almost two hours to complete the first seven holes an envoy was despatched from the British camp.

'Good morning, gentlemen, the Admiral with whom I am playing sends his compliments and wonders whether, as we are playing considerably faster than you, we might be allowed to play through?'

Four pairs of icy eyes bored into the Englishman, then a Brooklyn voice growled, 'My compliments to da Admiral. Tell him to get stuffed!'

China doesn't possess a golf course but on good authority there is at least one golf ball resident in the country. The authority is *Golf Digest*'s Frank Cox who visited China hoping to show the Chinese people something about golf.

Cox took along a few balls and a club that was supposed to telescope. The club wouldn't work properly and, besides, the Hong Kong customs wouldn't pass it anyway. Looking for a substitute club, Cox found a bamboo cane in Hangchow with a handle in the shape of a dragon that worked as a putter. Cox putted everywhere and attracted a lot of attention.

But he lost his cane just before he was to go to China's Great Wall and he was distraught. He'd wanted to hit a golf ball off the ancient wall — a 'first'.

One of Cox's fellow travellers, a woman from Houston, offered him the use of her collapsible metal cane, so Cox teed up a ball atop the wall and prepared for the historic shot. But when he swung, the cane broke into four pieces. Undaunted, Cox picked up the ball and heaved it over the wall's edge. Presumably it's still there, nestling in a really rugged lie.

There's no more sensitive moment for a golfer than when he is committed to his backswing — the point of no return where the slightest noise or interruption can wreck his concentration.

So golfers everywhere will have a tinge of sympathy for Dr Sherman A. Thomas of Washington, D.C., who was about to stroke a putt on the 17th green at the Congressional Country Club. At that precise moment a Canadian goose honked.

The good doctor missed his putt but not the goose, landing a telling blow on the unfortunate bird's head. Dr Thomas was charged in Federal court for killing a goose out of season.

The doctor maintained that he had merely committed euthanasia by dispatching the goose, which he claimed had been sorely injured by his approach shot. The Federal Magistrate thought otherwise; goosicide was the verdict, and Dr Thomas paid out a $500 fine.

We've heard of golfers putting 'bite' on the ball, but we've heard everything after the story of the golfer who was bitten by his own teeth.

It seems Joe Franzese's false teeth felt uncomfortable during a round at the Canajoharie Country Club, so he took them out, wrapped them in a handkerchief and put them in his back pocket. A few holes later a playing partner, Dick Hiller, heeled a shot and the ball whacked Franzese on that very pocket.

Franzese wasn't exactly hurt, but he checked his teeth and they were broken. The threesome then retired behind a bush to see if Franzese had sustained any further damage. Sure enough, he had been bitten by his own teeth.

Michael Green devoted his book, *The Art of Coarse Golf*, to those who are not only no good at the game, but who will never get any better ... the Coarse golfers of the world who habitually go from tee to green without touching the fairway, or who buy their tees one at a time.

This whimsical writer commenced one of his chapters thus: 'Watching a Coarse Golf party split up after their strokes is like sitting in the stalls at a Shakespearian history, when the King despatches his Lords to meet the rebels:

And thou good brother Warwick take the North
While our fair cousin Gloucester guards the South
And Essex hies himself unto the East
While we ourselves do hold the stormy West...

'Normally all players will march in opposite directions. It is not unknown for some to march forwards and others backwards if, for instance, a shot has rebounded from a shelter.

'Yet because a Coarse Golfer spends so much time in the rough he does have an opportunity for experiences which never come the way of better men. To him a golf course does not consist of a series of tees and greens linked by well-mown fairways, but of dense stretches of jungle. The Coarse Golfer wanders on the long summer afternoons through fern grot, rose plot and God wot. He knows the scent of the ragwort (whatever that is), the song of the plover, and the sweet, cloying smell of decaying dead animals.

'He knows, too, the meandering little streams which wind

'It was terrible, Inspector. My grip was all wrong. I lifted my head too early, bad follow-through ... '

their way through the woods and probably has invented his own names for some of nature's features, titles such as "Cockup Spinney", "Three-stroke Wood" and "Bastard Bushes".

'It is a strange sub-world, this life in the rough, and one which the better golfers miss. I sometimes feel sorry for a good golfer who can go round one of the most beautiful stretches of countryside in the world without ever leaving the deadly dull stretch of flat grass which comprises the fairway.

'Only the other week I watched two women golfers put their shots into a wood and vanish after them. "Women golfers", I sneered, and struck a firm, masculine stroke. The ball feebly dribbled into the same wood.

'When I went in there to search for it I found the women on their knees gathering flowers and chirping to each other like birds. "You always get such lovely primroses here", one of them told me, "but I think the bluebells in the wood by the 17th are nicer."

'Incidentally, it was a fascinating experience following those women round the course (I couldn't go through — I tried twice but kept putting the ball on the next fairway).

'Half the time they picked a club simply because they liked the colour of the grip. "Not that big club, Daphers", said the older woman. "Take the one with the pretty blue handle. It goes with your skirt". And they seemed completely impervious to all the normal emotions of golf.

'If they muffed a drive they didn't dance all over the tee in rage like any civilized human being but started worrying whether their cap was on straight. Getting into trouble didn't worry them at all, they seemed to regard the ball as a kindly guide leading them to interesting parts of the countryside.

'In fact, when young Daphers put her ball straight into the foulest morass in the south of England she positively jumped for joy and screamed, "Oh, I'm so glad it's gone there, we can see if those blackbirds have hatched out yet".

'But then that's women's golf all over. Don't believe that they are more emotional than men. It's the male who gets hysterical over that little white ball, it's the man who bursts into tears over his putts. Women don't really care — as long as their hair's not coming adrift.

'But to return to the rough. One of the blessings of being a Coarse Golfer is the interesting things that happen in there.

'Indeed, my friend Askew married a woman he met in the rough. At the height of summer he sliced a shot into a stretch of gorse and bushes and on going to search for the ball came upon a young woman in a deep sleep with the ball resting six inches from her head.

'Askew immediately claimed that the girl counted as a loose impediment and he was entitled to brush her away. I countered this by pointing out that loose impediments, according to the rules, include "dung, worms and insects, and casts or heaps made by them", and she didn't come into that category.

"In that case", said Askew, "she is young growth and I shall move two club lengths away".

'All might yet have been well but Askew is not at his best in a difficult lie and the girl was awoken, not by the sound of club hitting ball, but by the monotonous repetition of an obscene word, varied by occasional crackling of the undergrowth.

'Her first reaction was to give a shrill scream, to which Askew replied that he could well understand her being upset at seeing the rotten lie he was in, but not to worry, he had only taken five so far and there was still a chance of doing the hole in single figures if everyone would please keep quiet.

'They got married six months later, and now have been blessed with a daughter and a son whose real name I never know because Askew insists on referring to him as "Young Casual Water".

'For some time after the wedding Askew always used to doff his cap before he drove from the 3rd, but nowadays I notice that he is merely inclined to mutter something under his breath ...'

Sydney clubs exhort their members to carry sand buckets around the course to fill in divot holes. So when a large contingent of Japanese visiting golfers arrived at The Lakes, home professional John Sheargold urged them to take out buckets 'for the divots'. The Japanese returned after their round with their buckets dutifully crammed full of nice, fresh divots!

You won't find the Tumblewood Golf Club listed in any golfing directory which is a pity because, the way A.S. Graham rolls out his stories, it has to be the zaniest club of them all.

Graham is a founder member of Tumblewood G.C. and it's the hub of a book he's written with copious, hilarious cartoons. He spins a good yarn, too, as witness this extract from the House Committee's report:

'...vexing question of the lounge furniture.

'It was reported that once again bar takings were down, though consumption seemed to be up. An application from the Steward to build a new garage for his Jaguar was referred back.

'The professional has again brought up the question of the necessity for a trolley-shed, pointing out that he already has thirteen trolleys in his living room.

'Attention was drawn to the fact that some members are still using the roller towels, after having had showers. In view of the nasty accident to Major Jenkins who fell off a chair, it was decided to point out the danger of this practice.

'The Committee had once again to remind the Steward's wife that the drying room was for the benefit of members. Also in connection with the drying room, it was regretted that members still persisted in taking their drinks down there on cold days. The Secretary had reported finding what he thought was a bottle of stout spilled over his waterproof jacket.

'The condition of the draught beer, which had been the subject of some complaints from members, was looked into thoroughly by the whole Committee. It was decided that the complaints were groundless, and though the first pint or two tended to be cloudy, the beer was excellent right down to the bottom of the barrel.

'The lengthy investigation of the clubhouse main drains has now been completed, and we are pleased to report that the trouble has been traced to the Stilton in the dining-room.

'It was noted that the lock on the changing-room door...'

Mrs Wendy Egan fired a nine-hole round of 35 and told her Canberra dentist husband about it — repeatedly. Mr Egan listened patiently to the regular recounting shot-by-shot of the achievement and, in final desperation, inserted this ad. in the personal columns of the *Canberra Times:* 'My wife played her best round of golf last Tuesday. Would those who have not yet heard about it please phone 731103 for full details of every shot. Noel Egan.'

The first call came at 7 o'clock that Saturday morning and calls continued all week. Said Mrs Egan 'I must say it taught me a lesson'.

The setting was Birkdale on the Lancashire coast, the occasion was the British Open and the golf world chuckled over the greatest hoax ever perpetrated in the game.

We introduce Maurice Flitcroft, a forty-six-year-old crane driver from Barrow-in-Furness who had briefly taken up the game of golf and figured he would enter by the front door — the Open.

Flitcroft took his clubs, which he had bought through a mail-order firm, and entered under professional guise for the pre-qualifying rounds at the Formby Golf Club. His opening round was a card of 121 after which he decided not to go after the 36-hole mark because of such a bad start.

The crane driver confessed afterwards that he had not played a full round of golf until this outing at Formby.

'I felt the pressure of the big event', he said. 'I wasn't really

80

'It's obviously suicide ... look at his scorecard.'

ready for the championship. To be quite frank, I was a bit erratic. But I started to put it together towards the end of the round.' (He must have been referring to a par at the 14th, his only par of the day, resulting from a hooked tee shot, a hack back to the fairway and a skulled iron shot to three feet from the pin.)

Reporters asked him why he had picked the British Open for his first round of golf. 'I've been inspired by watching golf on telly', he replied. 'I sent away for a set of clubs through a mail-order firm and I started to practise on some fields at the back of our house. I am completely self-taught, you know. I've always been a bit of an athlete.

'Then I thought it would be nice to play in the Open with Jack Nicklaus and that lot. It would give me some encouragement. After all, I haven't reached my peak. Some of those top stars have been at it for years. They are well past their best.

'I'm going to improve and be back next year, and then watch out. And if I don't make it, then I'll take up painting. I'm quite a talented artist as well.'

Footnote: Flitcroft duly sent his entry a year later for the Open at St Andrews. The Royal and Ancient turned it down with the explanation that they were now empowered to demand evidence of ability. Stony silence greeted crane driver Flitcroft's plea that he had improved considerably and was prepared to give a demonstration of his ability around the Old Course at St Andrews.

Clive Clark, the British professional at Sunningdale, can turn his hand to a highly entertaining column. His encounters with tournament starters make delightful reading.

Clark relates his experience in the Australian PGA event some years ago. The field was sent on their way by a starter who stood on the first tee in an open-neck shirt and rather baggy pants which remained waist high due only to the tenacity of a pair of bright red braces. The starter zealously held on to the microphone like a kid who had just been given his first candy and had become an instant addict. Bet you've got one in your club. He always volunteers to do the auction!

Clark's experience continues: 'My playing partners that day were Peter Thomson and Gay Brewer. First away was Brewer.

"On the tee", announced the starter, "we have from the United States of America, Gay Brewer, winner of the Alcan Tournament, the U.S. Masters, the Pacific Masters, the Greater Greensboro Open and countless other tournaments. Ladies and Gentlemen, I give you Gay Brewer." Brewer hit a beauty.

"Next on the tee", continued the starter, "we have your very own favourite, Peter Thomson..." The gallery applauded again but they were shouted down, "...Twice winner of the New Zealand Open, five-time winner of the Australian Open". Thomson couldn't stand it any longer and smashed one down the centre while "red braces" was still in full throttle.

'Now it was my turn. "On the tee Clive Clark." I waited for a further announcement. Nothing happened. Not very charitable considering I had won two tournaments that year and had been third in the British Open. I addressed the ball and was just getting comfortable when he started again. "Clark, in 1967 tied for fifth place in the South African Pepsi Cola Tournament."

'The next day I arrived at the tee in time to hear the announcement of the first player of the threeball in front. "Next from Nationalist China, we have Cho Ling-low. He doesn't swing the scales far, but my word, would you watch him hit this one." Just imagine how Mr Cho is feeling. All of five-foot nothing and has just been proclaimed as one of the long hitters to swing a club! His drive had bounced three times before it dribbled into the 200-yard cross bunkers.

'It was at this stage that I decided I couldn't stand the inaccuracies of "red braces" any longer. I went over to him and had a few words. I explained that the day before I had been very disappointed that he hadn't mentioned my first achievement in golf. "I'm very sorry. What was it?" I told him.

'Again it was Brewer's honour and again we went through the entire ritual. Thomson looked extremely bored, and when it came to his turn he snubbed the man again by hitting off before the announcement was over.

'Now it was my turn. "Next on the tee from London, England, we have Clive Clark, who, in 1967 tied for fifth place in the South African Pepsi Cola Tournament. But his proudest moment surely came when he won the Glastonbury Sweetbreads."

'The gallery burst into laughter. If I'd known he was going to swallow that one, I'd have told him I'd won the Grand National.'

Clark recollects another starter encounter at a variety club Pro-Am outside London.

'I arrived on the tee and the starter introduced me and my partners. I teed off first and then my 10-handicap partner followed. We both hit good ones. The 12-handicap partner went and, though he connected quite well, his ball just missed the fairway.

'The last of the four was a 20-handicapper. From the number of quick waggles he made at the ball he was obviously nervous. At last, he got the club back. The gallery must have been wondering if it was ever going to happen. He took a quick flash at the ball which popped up into the sun and disappeared over some nearby tennis courts.

'My partner went to his caddie to reload, meanwhile one of the spectators, a lady, had assumed the ball had gone down the middle and was walking down the fairway.

'The starter yelled a blurting "fore", and then turning to me and shaking his head, said, "Who is that silly old bag?"

'Modesty almost prevented me from telling him that it was, in fact, my mother.'

'If we're still playing the 8th, it's about a couple of miles due east.'

Clive Clark maintains the worst thing that can happen to a starter is for him to get your name wrong. He thus not only shows to the gallery that he doesn't know what he's talking about, but he also stands a very good chance of getting a wedge between the ears.

At the Glen Campbell Los Angeles Open, the starter had either had too many the night before, suffered from severe myopia or had a typist of dubious talent.

Somehow the 'C' in Clive got joined up; he was announced as 'And next on the tee from London, England, we have Olive Clark'.

The pros never let Clive Clark forget that one!

Holding an angry goanna by the neck while your partner plays a recovery shot seems an unlikely story. But it happened at the Woodanilling course in Western Australia.

Miss Winifred Witham, honorary secretary of the Katanning Associates, recounted, 'We were playing as a three in a ladies open day competition at the picturesque little Woodanilling course. It was a bitterly cold, windy day, with light rain and sleet. Playing the last hole before lunch one of the ladies sliced her ball into a fallen tree area.

'Whereas I myself would have declared it unplayable, she and the other lady in our three decided to shift the branch of the fallen tree. This in itself was a mighty effort. There was the ball sitting beside a bob-tail goanna in its winter nest.

'So the other lady picked up the goanna and held it by the neck (she said that goannas were a farmer's best friend), while the owner of the ball got in and hit it well out on to the fairway. They put the goanna back in its nest, pulled the fallen branch back and left it in peace.'

Joe Kirkwood, the Australian golfer who won world acclaim for trick shots, handed out cards which carried this message:

Tell your story of hard luck shots,
  Of each shot straight and true,
But when you are done, remember son,
  Nobody cares but you.

Kirkwood claimed to have played 6,740 courses in his travels and he made a fortune playing exhibition trick golf, accompanying Walter Hagen on world tours.

He is said to have registered twenty-nine holes-in-one including one ace hit off the face of a watch, and a second at Sea Island, Georgia, while making a film. He was also the first professional to use a wooden tee peg.

Australia's oldest golfing trophy is the Cadogan Cup, presented way back in the misty year of 1884, and to this day the cause of tenacious rivalry among the members of the Australian Club, Kensington, NSW.

Such is the fame of the Cadogan Cup that it was flown to America to appear in a display of golf memorabilia in a gallery on Fifth Avenue. The *New York Times* light-heartedly questioned the effrontery of the 'land of the kangaroos' in actually having an established golf competition before any golf club had been formed in the United States.

Club historian, John Alenson, sifting through the colourful background of the Cadogan Cup, recounts one memorable occasion when the contest reached a pulsating climax. The outcome was not reached until the 18th green where the winning putt trembled on the edge of the hole before gently plopping into the cup.

The many spectators burst into a spontaneous round of applause and moved to congratulate the winner, only to see him supine on the green in a dead faint. So, instead of being traditionally chaired to the clubhouse on the shoulders of his supporters, he was ignominiously borne in a horizontal state to the locker room where medical aid soon restored him to complete recovery. It was reported, however, that very much later, after fully responding to the many toasts to his success, he assumed a similar position before his responsible friends 'saw him home'.

Peter Alliss is not only the world's ace golfing commentator and a former Ryder Cup player, he is a practical joker who takes some beating. Prudish readers should stop at this point.

Alliss and two close buddies, professional golfers Dave Thomas and Hugh Lewis, once shared a mild practical joke. Two of them planted a contraceptive in the baggage of the third so that it would reappear in slightly embarrassing circumstances when he got home.

The victim then had to retaliate but he also was obliged to advise the next victim, 'Noddy is hidden'. Thus tension mounted for the victim and delighted anticipation increased for the other two.

Thomas arrived on the tee one day to play an exhibition match. In front of a gallery he reached for his driver, pulled off the head cover and was appalled to see Noddy stretched over the clubhead. Hastily, he replaced the cover and drove off, instead, using his three-wood. The escapade continued with each man showing ever greater ingenuity in the chosen hiding place.

A truce was finally called after Peter Alliss' cunning had the other two all but nervous wrecks. It seems his final triumph occurred at a party with Thomas quietly sipping a gin and tonic in the midst of a group. Thomas glanced down at his drink and all but fainted. Alliss had frozen Noddy inside an ice cube, placed it in Thomas' glass and now it was mushrooming as the ice began to melt.

Oops! A British newspaper reporting the final of the national one-armed golfers' championship reported that the winner had grasped his opportunity 'with both hands' to beat the field!

American *Golf Digest* regularly features 'instant lessons' for its army of devoted readers.

One of these lessons urged each golfer to exert very light pressure on the club. It suggested that each player should imagine holding the club as lightly as if it were a tube of toothpaste with the cap off and he didn't want to squeeze any out.

A reader reported enthusiastically: 'Standing out there thinking about holding a toothpaste tube makes you relax all over. Your hands and arms don't tighten up, your shoulders turn easily and the whole swing just flows.'

But he added sadly that there was a resultant problem.

'When I started to brush my teeth next morning I couldn't bring myself to squeeze the toothpaste tube.'

St Andrews, historic home of the Royal and Ancient game, abounds in caddie stories.

An unfortunate American, at the close of an execrable match with a compatriot, found himself playing his fourth shot at the 18th still on the wrong side of the Swilcan burn. He topped it miserably into the water and, in his dismay, announced he was going to throw both himself and his clubs into the water and drown.

His caddie was unimpressed. 'You couldna', he snorted witheringly, 'keep your head down long enough'.

The 19th hole is the traditional place for story-telling and nobody can tell stories quite like golfers.

For instance, the account of the highly competent player who almost won his club title half a dozen times. On each occasion he came undone playing the 18th hole. Determined to overcome his horror of this unlucky finishing hole he turned up week after week and practised every conceivable type of shot until he was familiar with every blade of grass.

Championship day came round once again and he was under the card at the 17th but slumped with a disastrous 12 on his

'It was lucky it happened when it did really, it was my turn to buy the drinks.'

bogey hole, the 18th. As he holed his last putt he had a coronary and dropped dead.

Clubmates attended his cremation and his ashes, by request, were scattered across the fairway of the 18th. But just as the ashes were tossed into the air, a high gust of wind caught them and they were suddenly blown out of bounds!

The late Lou Allen of the Bonnie Doon club in Sydney always raised a chuckle with this story. Poker-faced he steadfastly claimed it was true.

Seems a member hooked his drive down into a grove of trees at the 15th hole. His playing partner, his wife, observed he was undecided how to go about the recovery shot.

'What do you plan to do?' she queried.

'I reckon I'll just chip out safely and play my third shot to the green. That way I could still get a par', he replied.

The wife countered, 'No. There's a small opening there between the trees. You might just get through and reach the green.'

Hubby accepted the advice but the ball ricocheted fiercely off a tree, hit the wife on the forehead and killed her.

A week later the same member playing the same hole again hooked his drive to finish in the same grove of trees.

His partner said, 'You're in a spot. How are you going to get out?'

The member said he reckoned the safest thing to do was to chip out onto the fairway.

His partner said, 'Heavens, no, there's an opening you could hit through and you might just get it up to the green'.

The member shook his head sadly and said, 'Not on your life. That cost me six shots here last week.'

The American professional, Doug Sanders, gleefully recounts the story of a girl caddie who worked for one of the touring professionals for a time on the circuit. All went well for two months until one day she burst into the lounge where the players were relaxing having a beer.

At the top of her voice, she called out, 'Hi, I have some bad news and some good news for you'.

'Cut it out', the pro said, 'I've just shot 83 and missed the "cut", so just give me the good news'.

'Sure', she said, 'the good news is that you're not sterile'.

The whackiest golf tournament ever played? Just listen to Sydney golfer Ted Ball's story of an hilarious event a handful of Australians contested back in 1963 in the Oklahoma township of Waco.

The event — the Waco Turner Open — was sponsored, organized and promoted by a gentleman called Waco Turner, an ageing Indian, reputedly earning $30,000 a day from the oil well he owned in the town of Waco.

Recounts Ted Ball: 'What was he doing running his own tournament? Well, it seems he was put out of a neighboring club because he wasn't wearing a tie, so he took great umbrage at this and decided to build his own golf course and conduct his own tournament.

'He did just that and his tournament got official status on the circuit.

'During construction of his course his workmen were drilling for water when they struck more oil. He promptly ordered them to plug the well and build a golfing green on top of it.

'Some features of the course included an airstrip for the boss's Cessna aircraft, a couple of ponds filled with fish to provide sport for the competitors, motel units and about six rusty Cadillacs shunted away in the greensheds. The Cadillacs, left out on the course, were believed to have run out of petrol and simply been abandoned where they stood. At the time of the tournament they were overgrown with grass.

'There were no outside spectators. Only Waco Turner's

92

closest friends and the caddies were welcome. Waco made the caddies a curious offer. At the end of each day's play they could earn themselves $1,000 if they cared to jump out of his Cessna plane into the course ponds. With the Cessna gliding at least 120 mph across the course the caddies, not unnaturally, found the offer easy to refuse. Waco raised the offer by $1,000 each day and I fancy he was unhappy that nobody took him up.

'On the first morning, one of the American contestants complained that his breakfast steak wasn't up to standard. When news got back to Waco Turner, the tournament sponsor turned up promptly with a loaded .45 revolver and asked the professional to leave. The pro disappeared quickly.

'Waco Turner, as I remember him, was a wiry, weather-beaten fellow who had all the appearance of an outback Australian shearer. I got on with him all right in our few meetings. But I had an unhappy experience with him on the final day.

'I was playing with Bruce Devlin and I was concentrating hard on a putt on the 70th green that could have tied the tournament lead for me.

'Suddenly Devlin said to me, "Hold it Ted, here comes Waco in his Cessna".

'Sure enough, Waco was dive bombing us from about 100 feet above. It's kind of hairy when you see a plane coming straight down at you.

'Gay Brewer won the tournament and I finished second, beaten by a shot. In all my tournament days I doubt I'm ever going to strike another like that one.'

Just another throwaway line from the one and only Lee Trevino, this time on his financial and physical fitness programmes: 'I want to be the richest guy and in the best shape of anybody in the cemetery when I die'.

Like a Holy Grail, golfers the world over strive for a magical hole-in-one. The odds against them? Well, you try and work them out.

The Salisbury Country Club, New York, in 1932 mustered 217 professionals and amateurs who all had previously scored 'aces'. This small army set out to achieve the feat again, each player hitting five shots, making a total of 1085 separate attempts. All failed and the nearest to the hole was 25 inches. Which suggests luck plays the major part in the golfing ace.

Harry Gonder, an American professional, in 1940 stood for 16 hours 25 minutes and hit 1,817 balls trying to hole out on a 160-yard hole. He had two official witnesses and caddies to tee and retrieve the balls and count the strokes.

The Golfers' Handbook records that the luckless Harry Gonder's first fifty shots took fifteen minutes to execute and his 86th shot finished 15 inches short. After playing 941 shots he stopped for some food. His 996th shot hit the pin and bounced three inches away. At 8.10 p.m. his 1162nd shot halted six inches short and his 1184th shot missed by three inches. At midnight he struck his 1600th shot.

He now had a severe blister on his hand and, after passing 1700, his hands began to throb and he could feel each shot up to the elbow. His 1750th shot struck the hole and came out and his 1756th shot did exactly the same thing, but stopped an inch from the hole. At 2.40 a.m. his 1817th shot stopped 10 feet from the pin and he then gave up his efforts.

The Golfers' Handbook lists I.S. South, a member of Highcliffe Castle Golf Club in England, as the oldest golfer to hole-in-one. He was 91.

The youngest is an Australian, Peter Toogood, son of a professional who holed out at Kingston's 110-yard seventh hole at the age of eight.

And if you doubt that luck's a fortune in the hole-in-one business, then we quote the case of Miss Gertrude Lawrence, distinguished actress, who, when playing golf for the first time, holed in one with her first tee shot.

'There used to be some quite nice countryside round these parts.'

A serious game golf might be, but its history is crammed full of zany contests and accomplishments.

Golfers have competed against anglers' casts, opponents using rackets, javelin throwers and archers. A player once backed himself to go round the links in 200 throws and won his bet.

But for a freak event, nothing surely touches the late Harry Dearth, a renowned vocalist, who played a round at Bushey Hall in a complete suit of heavy armour.

A Sonning professional, A.J. Young, in 1933 competed against a Captain Pennington who took part 'from the air'. Captain Pennington found the Sonning greens by dropping the balls as he circled over the course. The balls were covered in white cloth to ensure that they did not bounce once they struck the ground. The airman completed the course in forty minutes taking 29 'strokes'.

In 1914, at the start of World War I, J.N. Farrar, stationed at Royston, Herts, took a ten to one wager that he could go round Royston under 100 strokes equipped in full infantry marching order, water bottle, full field kit and haversack. Farrar made it in 94. His Commanding Officer was among the spectators.

The first lady golfer, mentioned by name, anyway, was Mary Queen of Scots.

As evidence of her indifference to the fate of Darnley, her husband who was murdered at Kirk o'Fields, Edinburgh, she was charged at her trial with having played at golf in the fields beside Seton a few days after his death. Mary was beheaded on 18 February 1587.

As Ian Wooldridge described it:'...his putt travelled 5,111 feet, a range from which even the immortal Jack Nicklaus has occasionally been known to miss'.

Wooldridge is sports columnist for the *Daily Mail* in London and has enjoyed sportswriter and columnist-of-the-year awards too numerous to mention.

His story of the longest putt in history delighted Londoners:

'Since Mr Trevor Nash is to big-time golf roughly what Mrs Margaret Thatcher is to the Kremlin netball team', he recounted, 'there will be those who resent the fact that he commemorated the dawn of 1977 by achieving the Most Remarkable Putt in History.

'Mr Nash, I should explain, is a buddy of mine with a 22 handicap, a swing like a Klondike lumberjack and a philosophy which maintains you might as well do it today because tomorrow you're more than likely to be struck by a Green Line bus.

'To be truthful it was at his third attempt—a deviation from the rigid code of rules laid down by the Royal and Ancient which I shall have to explain later—that Mr Nash holed out.

'Overcome by euphoric emotion he immediately called for several glasses of Dom Perignon '69 which were instantly served by a lady with good legs and a nice blue uniform. And really there was something to celebrate.

'For one thing, his putt travelled 5,111 feet, a range from which even the immortal Jack Nicklaus has occasionally been known to miss. For another, it sped along at almost 1½ times the speed of the average high velocity rifle bullet. Thirdly, it was accomplished 2,000 miles out over the Atlantic at an altitude approximately twice the height of Mount Everest.

'Some explanations are in order and the first is that with most of Britain greeting the New Year with an attack of almost terminal lethargy, Mr Nash and I contracted to relieve the boredom by playing a golf match with a small difference. The difference was that the first nine holes were to be played in Great Britain, the second nine holes were to be played in the United States of America and all 18 holes were to be negotiated in the same day.

'While this, during the brief dark days of a Northern

Hemisphere mid-winter, may appear to present certain logistical problems, nothing in fact could be more childishly simple. All you have to do is play the 2,992 yards that comprise the front nine holes at the Royal Mid-Surrey Club on the outskirts of London, hail a taxi to take you the nine miles between there and Heathrow, hop on a plane for the 3,778 mile ride to Dulles International Airport in Washington DC, hire a car for the 25-mile run to the military suburb of Arlington and then hack your way round the 3,356-yard back nine holes of America's Army-Navy Country Club.

'By the time you're through, you will have played 18 holes, par 70, over a course measuring 3,812 miles 1,068 yards from first tee to last green. You will also have accomplished it in a single span of daylight, which may just add up to the most meaningless record in the annals of mediocre amateur sport.

'Anyway, it was one way to start the year and the contestants are mutually grateful to the man who made it work: Captain Keith Myers, who belted British Airways fourth and newest Concorde, Alpha Delta, through head winds to cross the Atlantic in three hours, fifty-six minutes. Concorde's speed, in conjunction with the five-hour time difference between Greenwich and Washington, actually meant that we were landing sixty-four minutes before we were due to take off.

'At 8.50 a.m., London time, we were driving off at Royal Mid-Surrey, which is bounded by Kew Gardens on one side and some distinctly plebeian municipal planning on the other, on the very terrain where the late Edward VIII took his problems when he was trying to grapple with the constitutional impasse which decreed he could have the Throne or Mrs Simpson but definitely not both.

'At 3.58 p.m., Washington time, we were hitting off at the Army-Navy Country Club which is within mortar range of The Pentagon and just down the hill from John F. Kennedy's grave, at a course whose membership in recent years has included such contrasting luminaries as Richard M. Nixon,

Lyndon B. Johnson and JFK himself. Unfortunately, the world being the shambles it is, none of them was permitted to play there during his Presidential term since one corner of the course is overshadowed by high-rise buildings from which even the most astigmatic assassin could not have missed a man stooped in concentration over a putt.

'Its most famous Old Boy, therefore, remains Dwight D. Eisenhower who played there as a cadet, General, Supreme Commander and President, and bequeathed to the club his gaudy old red and blue golf bag and a full set of irons. These are impaled on a wall and testify to Dwight D's eternal self-effacement. The five stars of his military rank are not only plastered in gold all over the golf bag but engraved on the heads of each of the clubs as well.

'However, the Eisenhower spirit prevails. With Washington whitefaced and shivering at 27 degrees F. all the golf courses were closed except the Army-Navy Club where words such as defeat, withdrawal and adversity are unknown. "It's our pleasure", said Mr Steve Tobash, professional, as he directed us to the 10th tee.

'Since tactics on both sides of the Atlantic were never to hit the ball out of sight on fairways patch-worked with snow, frost and ice, the hole-by-hole scores will be treated as classified information for the next thirty years. It is sufficient to record that we stood all-square on the ninth green at Royal Mid-Surrey, measured out the lengths of our respective putts, measured out the same distance in Concorde when it reached level flight at 59,000 feet and proceeded to complete the hole by putting up the gangway into a champagne glass. This was how Trevor Nash, at the third attempt, achieved the Most Remarkable Putt in History.

'In the 2½ seconds it took his ball to travel along 45 feet of red carpet, Concorde itself, travelling at slightly more than 1,300 miles an hour, had rolled a further 5,066 feet towards Washington.

'Mr Nash, as it happens, lost the match two-and-one but

'I've never seen a chap take so much trouble over his putting.'

that was the least of his setbacks. In the extremely expensive bar of an extremely expensive hotel that evening an American lady of indeterminate vintage but claiming to be a Basque whose many marriages had included one to the Count von Essen, asked him how he'd spent the day.

"Playing golf", said my mate.

"Oh", huffed the Countess. "How stupendously boring." '

No doubt about it, Arnold Palmer has been one of the most idolized figures in the whole history of American sport. His magnetism among golf followers is legendary. The fans followed him in their thousands. Critics dubbed them 'Arnie's Armies'.

Here are two letters from unknown admirers which sum up the Palmer appeal.

Dear Mr Palmer,

I watched you play in the Western Open. I am not sure if you will ever read this letter but at any rate during the Western Open on the 8th tee my buddy and I got one of the cigarettes that you threw away after you had finished with it. We cut it in half and split it and my buddy got the filter tip and stitched it onto the back of his golf glove. However, I got the other part of the cigarette and when I tried to stitch it on, it just fell apart and crumpled up and I wonder if you would by any chance please send me another cigarette butt.

Dear Mr Palmer,

A couple of weeks ago, you were gracious enough to interrupt your dinner and come over and shake the hands of a group of us who were also dining. First of all, I want to thank you again for taking the time and trouble to do this. I would imagine that it sometimes becomes quite a nuisance to be so well known.

The sequel to the story is that none of us washed our hands

for the next 24 hours and rushed out to the golf course the next day to see what magical effect this handshake might have had on us. Apparently I was the only one tuned in to the proper wave length as I came in with an 81 with a triple bogey and two double bogeys. This was extremely gratifying to a struggling 15-handicap golfer.

If you can find some way to package some of this magic and send it along to me, I'll be delighted to send you all of my future winnings. Good luck to you in future play and thanks again from all of us.

Arnie, of course, never lacked advice, even when his putter went sour and he experienced lean years.

Dear Mr Palmer,
You place the club a half inch behind the ball. Now here is the big, new idea. You absolutely stare at the space between the ball and the club. Do this until you get it firmly fixed in your consciousness...

Dear Mr Palmer,
I have been playing golf for about forty years, and now that I am getting older my timing gets off. The other day I went out to hit some practice balls and for some reason I started humming 'The Volga Boatman'. In a short while I was hitting with the rhythm of my humming and my swing and timing fell together...

Bob Hope's passion for golf is well known. He even promotes his own tournaments in America and Britain. His own claims to golfing prowess, however, suggest he's no great shakes. Certainly Arnold Palmer didn't boost his ego with this exchange of quips when the pair took part in a television show in 1963.

HOPE: Arnie, you've probably made as much money out of golf as any man in history.

PALMER: Don't you believe it, Bob. Sam Snead's got more buried underground than I ever made on top.

HOPE: I wondered why he liked to go barefoot. I thought that was just a story.

PALMER: No, sir, he's got gophers in his backyard that subscribe to *Fortune* magazine. He's packed more coffee cans than Brazil.

HOPE: Where does he get all the loot?

PALMER: Pigeons! Amateurs that think they can beat him.

HOPE(to audience): Why is he staring at me?

PALMER: Ever play Snead, Bob?

HOPE: Sure. But I almost beat him. I was even until the last hole when we doubled the bet. (Realization.) Hey, wait a minute! You don't mean... he...

PALMER: Welcome to the flock.

HOPE: If I ever find one of his gophers, I'm gonna turn him upside down and shake him until I get my half-dollar back. Since we're being so commercial, how come you never invited me to appear on 'Challenge Golf'?

PALMER: We don't do comedy, Bob.

HOPE: I mean to play golf.

PALMER: We don't do comedy, Bob.

HOPE: Let's get down to your business and my pleasure. You don't mind having your brain washed?

PALMER: At these prices you can shampoo it, dry and set it!

HOPE: You're too generous. Okay, what's wrong with my game?

PALMER: If you're talking about golf, that's not your game.

HOPE: I think my golf is sound.

PALMER: It is. Talk, talk, talk!

HOPE: They tell me I have a picture swing.

PALMER: True. I saw your last picture. Fun-nee!

HOPE: My short game is good.

PALMER: That's right. Unfortunately your short game is off the tee.

HOPE: My putting?

PALMER: Like your act. Once in a while you get a good line.

HOPE: Enough of this levity, let's get down to business. (Picks up club.) What do you think of my swing? (Demonstrates.)

PALMER: I've seen better swings in a condemned playground.

HOPE: That's a studied swing. Don't I remind you of somebody?

PALMER: Yes.

HOPE: Souchak? Snead?

PALMER: No.... the Little Old Winemaker.

HOPE (to audience): I could have gotten Cary Middlecoff for the same money and had my teeth checked.

The big, beefy professional from the Catalina Club, Bateman's Bay, stepped up on the tee for the staging of the 1972 Wills Masters. The starter slotted his name on the board: RICHARD BEER.

The gallery gave a laugh when the second professional to hit off moved on to the tee. His name: STEWART GINN.

There was an absolute howl of delight when the third member of this professional trio took his place on the tee. His name: PHIL CHURCH.

Beer, Ginn and Church! The promoters, just a trifle red-faced, maintained doggedly it had all been an accident. No mischief was intended.

The passion that golfers nurture for this odd game was never better illustrated than at the Sydney club of Avondale.

Club member, Max Meale suffered a heart attack as he hit a

'Bet he never did find his ball.'

very long putt on the 18th green. He fell to the turf before the ball dropped into the hole.

When Max came to in hospital, he asked his wife, 'Did I get the putt?' When she said that indeed he had, he replied, 'Good, I might win a ball'.

He died the following day.

The beloved Henry Longhurst's army of readers regularly forgave him his moments of aberration. The matchless, good-humoured Longhurst began his Sunday column on one occasion:

'Not having been home this week, I do not yet know the number of correspondents who have written to point out my chivalrous inaccuracy last Sunday in giving the English women golfers a victory in the first "World Tournament" held recently at St Germain, Paris, when, in fact, they finished third behind France and America — which, now I come to think of it, I knew perfectly well.

'These things happen and I am only thankful that I got it wrong the right way, so to speak, and did not say they were third when in fact they were first.'

Diminutive British golfer Guy Hunt seemed poised for all sorts of conquests. He had won Ryder Cup and World Cup selection and had earned an invitation to the Masters.

But suddenly his game went sour and all because he was drawn to play alongside Lee Trevino.

Trevino was astonished to see Hunt spitting on the clubface of his driver before each tee shot. Trevino pointed out that in the extreme, it could be considered an artificial device that the Royal and Ancient lawmakers might not approve. The official word followed that Hunt should stop it.

Hunt said his spitting habit was a mixture of superstitious ritual and a personal theory that the spittle gave the clubface better adhesion to the ball and produced a straighter shot. He stopped doing it and his game went downhill.

Poor Hunt. He was last seen desperately striving to put a new spit and polish to his game.

A puzzled club golfer watched a fellow member don some unorthodox gear in the locker-room.

'How long have you been wearing a corset?' he asked.

'Ever since my wife found it in the car', was the reply.

The Bing Crosby Pro-Am at Pebble Beach has been a highlight of the American golfing year, so much so that following Bing's death, his son, Nathaniel, elected to keep the popular event going.

Bing used to invite the amateurs, many of them celebrities and some very good golfers among them, too. When one top company executive failed to respond to his invitation, Bing himself got on the telephone to him.

Crosby recounted afterwards, 'He didn't believe it was me no matter how hard I tried to convince him. He said he knew it was one of his friends pulling his leg. Finally, I had to sing the first few bars of White Christmas.'

Vincent Tshabalala is a black Johannesburg motor mechanic who pined for the chance to play professional golf. He got that chance thanks to Gary Player, who sponsored him on a world tour.

The experience paid huge dividends and Vincent responded by winning the French Open championship a couple of years later. He won a useful first-prize cheque of $5,500 but was more enthusiastic about the prize that the West Rand Bantu Golf Union had prepared for him. A goat!

Said Vincent, 'It is one of our customs. It's a great honour, I can tell you.'

The Norfolk Island Golf Club has passed its 50th birthday. The course is a scenic nine-hole layout bounded on three sides by the Pacific Ocean. The clubhouse is a restored Georgian house built during the second convict settlement on Norfolk Island. Greens are protected from grazing cattle by wire fences.

And once a year the Island holds a race meeting with the field thundering down the last fairway, which serves as the straight, to pass the clubhouse, which is the finishing line!

Bob Hope once said, 'I'd give up golf like a shot— it's just that I've got so many sweaters'.

Hope visited The Lakes Club on one Australian tour and spied in the professional shop a natty golfing hat complete with a compass. He promptly bought it and said he'd be presenting it to another golfing nut, the former U.S. president, Gerald Ford.

Hope said, 'He's one guy who really needs a compass. Last time he went out he collected four moose, three elk and a mason.'

The 19th is the traditional watering hole for weary golfers and the place where many a good story is spun. Like the tale of a Keysborough member who holed a chip shot, went to recover his ball and found the cup was already occupied. He told his audience that a baby possum was curled around the bottom of the flagstick.

But this storyteller was upstaged by a Mornington golfer who assured his listeners that he had hit a magpie in full flight. And he swore he could produce the ball with the luckless bird's beak still embedded in the cover to prove it!

New Zealand's most unusual local rule is located on the wall of the Rakauroa Club, 2000 feet into the hills of the province of Poverty Bay.

The rule provides that if a shot comes to rest within six feet of a new-born lamb, the ball can be dropped.

As befits a majestic layout, Royal Canberra over the years has attracted the attentions of Australia's prime ministers, who have provided their own enchanting chapter in the club's history.

The first of our golfing prime ministers was Stanley Melbourne Bruce, whose father, J.M. Bruce, is one of two men credited with effectively establishing golf in Victoria in 1881.

On 10 December 1927, Mr Bruce drove the first ball officially to open the full 18-hole Canberra golf links, six years before King George V gave it royal status.

In a subsequent salute to golf, Mr Bruce said in a farewell speech after losing the prime ministership, 'I could not have remained prime minister for nearly seven years and retired feeling as fit as when I began, had it not been for the fact that I have played golf. If all the prime ministers who are going to succeed me can play golf they will last for a reasonable time— but if they do not play they will not last very long. Some people are under the illusion that you have to have brains to be a prime minister but the great qualification is an amazing amount of physical strength, and the only way to maintain it is to play golf.'

William Morris Hughes pursued the golf ball from the 1920s almost until his death in the 1950s. He had a reputation as an indefatigable ball-searcher. One of his partners, tiring of the long search in the rough, dropped an almost new ball into a tussock and shouted, 'Here you are, Mr Hughes, here it is'.

Billy examined the ball carefully, decided it wasn't his,

pocketed it, and resumed his search for another five minutes.

Jim Scullin was no golfer, though he was photographed in the gardens of Parliament House with the great Walter Hagen and Australia's Joe Kirkwood during their 1930 barnstorming tour of Australian courses.

Mr J.A. Lyons became a golfing addict and a newspaper report on 1 October 1935 recorded:

'The Prime Minister has no pretensions as a golfer, but he made history on the Royal Canberra links today. When playing from the 15th tee across the Molonglo River, he topped the ball, which drove on to the water, ricocheted, and landed on the green, enabling him to hole out for a par three. The muddy bottom of the Molonglo at this point is studded thickly with the offerings of players whose drives have failed to carry the only water hazard on the links.'

Sir Robert Menzies proclaimed that his sporting interests were 'watching cricket' and 'walking (without the distraction and emotional stress attaching to the pursuit of the incorrigible small white ball)'.

St Andrews, ancestral home of golf, has been slipping into the North Sea at the rate of a foot a year since the 1960s. But man's ingenuity, particularly golfers', will surely stem such coastal erosion.

After all, back in the nineteenth century Sir Hugh Lyon Playfair, captain of the Royal and Ancient and Provost of St Andrews, reclaimed land that is now the mutual fairway between the first and 18th holes. Sir Hugh was a practical fellow who took the precaution of having his umbrella inscribed 'Stolen from Major Playfair'.

St Andrews is all things to all golfers. Golf at St Andrews dates back to the twelfth century and provides the game with

110

'Great news ... I'm down to a 12 handicap!'

its most famous folklore. In 1885 a St Andrews student, R.F. Murray, penned these lines:

The city boasts an old and learned college,
Where you'd think the leading industry was Greek;
Even there the favoured instruments of knowledge,
Are a drive and a putter and a cleek.

The Old Course is shaped like a shepherd's crook, straight out and straight back, save for the loop, and a succession of double greens have replaced the original small greens. So huge are their surfaces that the American Doug Sanders once said he preferred Birkdale 'because when you putt there you don't have to pivot'.

At one time there were 22 holes on the Old Course but four were eliminated and thus 18 holes became standard for golf, quite by accident.

Women have been barred down the centuries from the great grey stone clubhouse but in 1975 the Royal and Ancient threw open the doors on the occasion of the British Women's Championship. The members and staff did their best to behave as normal but the feeling, according to one critic, was rather that of occupied France in one of those wartime films.

The critic added, 'Not, of course, that the Ladies Golf Union are quite the Gestapo even if, as one unchivalrous soul suggested, the average male might well be no less frightened of their midnight knock on the door'.

We golf columnists voted way back in 1974 the golf shot of that year belonged to Nigel Denham, who got out of trouble in the English Amateur at Moortown with a deft 10-iron shot. Denham had overclubbed at the 18th and the ball had disappeared through a doorway into the men's bar.

The clubhouse not being out of bounds, Denham had the option of declaring his ball unplayable or of opening a window and pitching out on to the adjacent green. To the astonishment and admiration of the crowded bar he played out through the window onto the green and just missed his par.

It's nice to report that he conformed to clubhouse rules by removing his spiked shoes before playing his window recovery shot.

The venue of the British Open Championship moves round each year on a rotation system. In 1977 the R and A broke new ground when they took the Open to Turnberry, a testing links course on the Ayrshire coast of Scotland. The course is owned by British Railways. During the war the RAF Coastal Command flattened the fairways to build concrete runways but British Railways restored the old golf course in the post-war years.

The caddies included such romantically named characters as Long John, the Wasp, Happy and the Lawyer. The ninth green sits alongside a lighthouse and an American visitor casually asked his caddie if the lighthouse still worked.

'Yes, sir, but only at night', replied the caddie.

Lee Trevino admits to being a frustrated cricketer at heart. He came to Sydney on one trip and delighted the gallery by giving a demonstration on the tee, polishing his golf ball on the side of his slacks and loping along the tee to deliver what looked like a creaky sort of leg-spinner. Then he played a few imaginary pushy shots, just like Bill Lawry playing the rock.

'Man I love that cricket', he said recalling how he watched cricket on television during visits to Britain. 'I just want to see the guy with the ball knock the wicket down. There was this time when I was watching and my wife asked me to get her a glass of water. Damned if the guy didn't knock everything down and by the time I got back with the glass of water they had fixed them all up again.'

Trevino sighed, 'Man, I've just got to play some of that cricket.'

Johnny Miller, for a year or two the golden boy of American golf, took up duck hunting as a leg strengthening exercise. He discovered it was very exciting.

'The way I shoot, the ducks have a heckuva chance', he said. 'It's sport for them and me, too.'

Sports Illustrated reported that scoring a hole in one in Japan can be a costly experience. None of that round of drinks stuff; a lavish geisha party at least.

An enterprising businessman established the Nippon Hole-in-One Club to insure members at $2.51 against the likely cost of $2,500 for a celebration payout. The club management worked on the statistics of one in every 1,000 players scoring the magic ace.

In the first year, 54 of the 12,000 members did. The Nippon Club went bankrupt.

You've got to admit, pro golfers have got a flair for the colourful in their quotes. Like big Jim Dent, the most spectacular hitter on the American circuit. He's long, mighty long, but not always accurate. Says Dent, 'I can airmail the golf ball, but I don't always put the right address on it'.

Old trouper Gene Sarazen concedes that in the modern day multi-million-dollar circuit, the pros are fitter than in the old days. 'They keep in better shape running to the bank', he says.

Carol Mann reckoned that the men's pro tour has peaked and the women's tour is taking over. Why? 'Legs.'

American golfer, Larry Ziegler looked back on an unhappy and highly unfinancial year on the U.S. tour. He quipped, 'I played so bad I got a get-well card from the Internal Revenue Service'.

Come to think of it, amateurs can be pretty colourful, too. Like red-bearded Irish playwright and actor, Patrick McCarville, who watched his opponent hit to a par-three green and mumbled to his caddie, 'Is the gentleman in the bunker or is the bastard on the green?'

Golf Digest's Dick Emmons offered his readers this 'inside information':

All crocodiles eat golf balls
For breakfast, lunch and snacks —
Which makes it plain how they obtain
Those knobs upon their backs.

The Governor of Victoria, Sir Henry Winneke, sire of some bouncing VFL footballers, is a dedicated golfer. At a tournament players' dinner in Melbourne he humorously related this spirited exchange during one of his social fourballs.

It seems that one member of his team strayed into the rough where he located his ball, stooping over to identify it. As he bent over he was struck firmly on the rump by another ball. Looking back he perceived a woman golfer who had just completed her swing. Obviously satisfied that she was the culprit, he strode back up the fairway and said peevishly, 'Madam, would you kindly aim at the hole with the flag in it'.

Marauding crows were creating havoc among Wollongong club golfers. Two young members hit off and the crows duly swooped down the fairway and made off with the balls. A club old-timer in the group promptly pulled out a bottle of eucalyptus oil, gave his ball a rub before hitting off and turned to his young partners saying, 'Won't you young fellows ever learn?'

To his dismay, however, he turned round to see a crow return to seize his ball, too.

'What have you got to say, now?' one of the young members asked.

The old-timer countered defensively, 'He must have had a cold'.

More about irascible old Tommy Bolt who confesses he would have liked to have rid himself of that temperamental title they hung on him 'way back'.

Says Bolt, 'I'd like to have gotten rid of that title but this here is a game the Pope would get mad at. I might have done it if I had worked at controlling my emotions. Actually, I work harder at it now than I did in my younger days. In comparison, take a nice easy guy like Jack Nicklaus. He never had anything to get mad about and I'm happy for him. But there's a tremendous difference between a silver spoon and trying to eat soup with a tin fork.'

Poor Tommy. He won the United States Open back in 1958, and actually behaved himself. Well, almost. He didn't try any javelin record throws with his clubs ('Always throw them forward, pard', he would advise) and he kept his cool for four rounds. But then he read a Tulsa newspaper which gave his age as 49 when it was only 39. He burned at that.

The newspaper's representative apologised and pleaded that it was a misprint, a typographical error.

'Typographical error my eye', blazed old Tommy. 'It's a perfect four and a perfect nine.'

Okay, so why is Nancy Lopez arguably the greatest woman golfer of all time? She reveals that deer hunting has been a major factor in her success. Nancy says everyone reckons the best part of her game is judgement of distance.

'I've got my dad to thank for that', she says. 'He took me on hunting trips almost as soon as I could walk. I had to sight the deer and judge the distance. We were poor and bullets were expensive so there was no second guessing.'

At Myrtle Beach, California, they introduced a novel tournament, the Big and Tall Golf Classic. You have to be at least 6ft 2 in tall and weigh in over 200 pounds (14 st. 4 lbs) to get a start. Some 54 players teed it up for the first tournament, totalling 340 feet and 11,000 lb of golfers on the hoof.

When Jack Nicklaus won the Australian Open in 1978 it was little short of a miracle. Not ability-wise, just that a few days earlier Jack had wrestled for more than six hours through the night with a giant marlin off the Barrier Reef. His arms and shoulders ached for days afterwards.

The marlin was the biggest caught that year, weighing in at 1,358 lbs, and a triumphant Nicklaus had it mounted and encased in a huge box to be sent to America for display in the clubhouse of a course he was designing.

In the meantime, the marlin took pride of place over a stone fireplace in Nicklaus's Florida living room. The huge fish's five-foot fin stuck out intimidatingly.

Nicklaus recalled, 'The marlin's fin had my wife, Barbara, so worried she stuck a red flag on it so that nobody passing by would kill himself'.

Comedian Bob Hope has celebrated his 50th year as an active golfer and his 20th year as sponsor of the Bob Hope Desert Classic. *Golf Digest* paid Hope a tribute and said the showbiz giant had played an estimated 2000 courses around the world with presidents, kings, generals, tycoons, actors and singers.

Did you know that Hope, born in Eltham, England, shot pool and worked as a delivery boy and a fountain clerk as a youngster? He boxed under the name of Packy East, the name that still identifies his locker at Lakeside Club in America.

Hope earned millions of dollars for charity, playing golf with the late Bing Crosby.

But his favourite partner was Jimmy Demaret. Standing on

the 10th at Pebble Beach, he once asked Demaret, 'Can I get home from here?'

'I dunno', said his partner. 'Where do you live?'

Hope was awed by Demaret's control over the ball in high winds. 'I think he was born in the wind. His mother had to run five miles to retrieve him', quipped Hope.

American Jerry Heard, a regular visitor on the Australian circuit and winner of our Open, these days swigs enthusiastically from a mystery bottle. A bachelor again after seven years of marriage, Heard shares a home-base in the Valley of the Moon, in California vineyard territory. And he's discovered a spring spewing water from lava rocks. After calling in a Swiss chemist to make tests, he's bottling the stuff commercially.

Says Heard, 'It really gives me a lift. It has twice the amount of oxygen as normal water and is just great for hangovers.'

The perfect round of golf? Nobody has ever played it, of course. Ben Hogan once recounted that he had dreamt he had birdied the first 17 holes in a row, then that his birdie putt at the 18th had lipped out. He woke up feeling furious with himself.

Australia's Peter Thomson, five times winner of the British Open, had a laugh at the expense of a zealous non-golfing press agency man on the eve of the British Open at Birkdale. The agency man followed Thomson after his practice round, bailed him up and asked how he had hit the ball.

Thomson replied, 'Son, I played the perfect round. I putted the ball to all the spots where the cups are going to be placed in the first round tomorrow and they all went in!'

'That's pretty good', commented the bemused agency follow.

'Yes', said Thomson, 'but maybe it wouldn't be a good idea to print it'.

Thomson is renowned as much for his dry humour as for his superlative golf.

He grappled with the tough Kori grass of Japan in one Asian tournament, leaving a crucial putt six feet short.

'Isn't this the toughest grass you've ever seen?' he asked his playing partner and fellow countryman, Graham Marsh. 'It would choke a goat!'

Graham Marsh, recalling his early days on tour, once shared a humble hotel room with the South African, Simon Hobday.

'Time to do some washing', remarked Hobday, with which he emptied a complete suitcase full of clothes into a previously filled bath. Then he pulled out a five-iron from his golf bag and swished the washing around until he was satisfied it was all clean.

Western Australia celebrated their 150th birthday with a $150,000 Open golf championship. A grand for every year. The venue was the bush setting of Lake Karrinyup Club. There was consternation when a patch of marihuana was discovered at the back of the 15th green. The famous cartoonist, Rigby, saw the humour of it all and next day had his newspaper readers chuckling with a scene depicting two kangaroos standing at the back of a golf gallery both smoking pot.

Two hardy campaigners of the Australian circuit, Alan Murray and Lindsay Sharp, still shudder a little when they recall an experience in their early tour days that landed them in a police cell. The pair had contested a pro-amateur event at Townsville in which one of their amateur partners was a local horse trainer. He assured them he had a 'certainty' on the job. at the race-track next day. Murray and Sharp were so impressed that they plunged both their tournament winnings and their modest holdings on the 'certainty'. They watched it cross the line with another horse and were mortified to see the judge give his verdict against them.

Penniless, they took to the highway next morning and finally were offered a ride by a friendly motorist. They hadn't gone far before they realized their host was well under the weather. He weaved back and across the highway as though beset by a combined hook and shank disease. The pair gratefully bailed out at Ayr. But there wasn't another hitch in sight. Night fell, the cold set in and the pair huddled on the side of the road, pulling a sheet of plastic over them to find some warmth. The police found them in the early morning.

The gendarmes listened sympathetically to their story and finally gave them sanctuary in the local police cell. A few hours later, they organized the two golfers a lift in a footballers' bus to Mackay where they were due on the tee for the next pro-amateur. They made it in the nick of time. Alan Murray, without any sleep, drove off and won the event to replenish a desperately empty purse.

Norman von Nida, pound for pound, or is it kilo for kilo? — our greatest ever Australian golfer, developed 'Popeye' arms as a youngster employed in a Queensland abattoir. His job was to break sheep heads open after they had been partially split by machines.

The Von grew up in a poor family and with limited education. There was no spare cash and he earned some pocket money as a bare-foot caddie on the nearby Royal Queensland Golf Club.

The first golf ball he hit was with a borrowed cleek, but his expeditions invariably ended with the course ranger roughly escorting him off the course. When Norman was eleven years of age, one of the club members, Dr George Thomson, saw his potential and gave him the use of his clubs. At 12, von Nida shot 86 to become the clubs's number one caddie.

He stood knee-high to a grasshopper but when the exalted American, Walter Hagen, made his first visit to Brisbane in 1929 to give an exhibition, the Von stepped up for the caddying job. Hagen looked surprised at the undersized youngster.

Von Nida spoke up: 'That's all right, Mr Hagen. I am to carry your clubs. I am the best caddie in Brisbane.'

Hagen looked down at him and said, 'O.K., son, then you and I are a pair because I'm the best golfer in Brisbane'.

Von Nida received £10 for his toil. Eight years later he defeated the great Walter Hagen one-up after a thrilling thirty-six hole match on Brisbane's Indooroopilly and Gailes courses!

Beauty, as they say, is in the eye of the beholder. Mount Osmond, located some four miles from the Adelaide Post Office as the crow flies, boasts a superlative view of the city from its 1,300 feet lofty station in the hills. The course is rugged going, tough climbing, steep slopes. One sportswriter branded it a course for mountain goats. Mountain goats indeed! World traveller, author and raconteur, Alf Bertram, penned these enthusiastic lines:

'This is golf amidst celestial spheres, a muted Aeolian harp echoing through the veiling fog, an ecstatic paean of welcome when a small white ball drops gratefully into a nectarized cup nestling in a velvet sward.'

Australians love the proverbial battler. Certainly Kel Nagle had no silver spoon in his youth. He tried his hand at dairy farming and carpentry as his family struggled to survive the Depression years. Later he had to duck the occasional bomb at Darwin and the falling coconut at Moratai during the World War II years.

Nagle matured late in the game of professional golf. But the best things come to those who wait and the ever popular Kel enjoyed his greatest triumph in his fortieth year. He had been playing in the United States and a whim took him into a golfing warehouse at Fort Worth, Texas. He pulled out a new driver, fiddled with the club and suddenly had a conviction this was for him.

'If you had told me to hit to the left, or the right, or down the middle, I could have done it with this driver,' he said.

Peter Thomson, his great travelling mate, told him he was hitting the ball so well with the driver that he could go on and win the British Open. Nagle did just that. He won the Centenary Open at golf's ancient home, St Andrew's, surviving a third day wash-out and negotiating the last hole, the Valley of Sin, to get the par that clinched the title a shot ahead of Arnold Palmer.

'Winning was just fantastic', he agreed afterwards. 'When you run second it doesn't seem to mean a thing. In golf you are remembered on records and history.'

They say that no champion has ever swung the golf club so simply as Peter Thomson. He has never written a book on technique, claiming that it could all be put into a couple of sheets of paper. At that, most of the instruction would centre about setting up.

The critic, Pat Ward-Thomas, wrote of Thomson, 'I never saw a golfer who seemed so assured of his destiny. There is about him an unmistakable air of success...'

Some of the Thomson simple philosphy:

• Anyone who can walk can play golf. It is a walking game. To be a good golfer you must be a good walker; you must condition your legs.

• Walking with a steady, relaxed rhythm, arms swinging freely, will help your game.

• A light, tender, sensitive touch is worth a ton of brawn.

• You think best when you are happiest.

• You can tell when a golfer is thinking freely. He goes along with his head up and a happy attitude.

- Sucess in golf is 50 per cent what you do and 50 per cent what other people do. So remember that they may not be doing their 50 per cent as well as you are doing yours. Stay calm and alert and recognize your opportunities.
- You have to like and enjoy what you are doing and where you are doing it. It is a good idea to make up your mind to like a course you are about to play, to like the people you are playing with, and to enjoy the weather, hot or cold!

Golf is renowned as a game for people from eight to eighty. Then what about Leigh Winser, the astonishing Barwon Heads stalwart who is now in his mid-nineties, still playing regularly and just as consistently beating his own age with his scoring.

Son of a Cheshire minister, he was a cricketing team-mate of S.F. Barnes and once played against the immortal Dr W.G. Grace.

Yes, Leigh Winser is still going strong, which is quite a story because in 1909 his father sent him to Adelaide to work on an apple orchard in the nearby Mount Lofty ranges. Why? Because he was 'the sickly member of the family'.

Henry Cotton, Britain's golfing maestro, recently wrote a book called *Thanks for the Game* and he spiced it with some wonderful anecdotes. Not surprisingly, he made some extraordinary friendships through golf. The most unusual of them all, surely, occurred in 1956 when he decided to have one more crack at the Masters at Augusta and the U.S. Open. In the mail came a hundred dollar bill and a request for advice on a golfing problem or two.

This is the amazing story Cotton recounted:

'The letter was from somebody I had never met: Colonel J.B. Kaine of Chicago, who turned out to be a city banker, 69 years old, and a golf 'nut' of the first order.

'I replied saying: "I do not think I can justify your generosity by a few words in a letter, not knowing you personally,

123

but on my way to play in the Masters I will be in New York for a couple of days. So I will contact you and see if we cannot get together at some point in my trip, where I can see you hit shots and probably help you."

'My ship was on time. I arrived at the St Regis Hotel, the bell boys had just carried up the baggage and I was dishing out dollar bills like pamphlets as tips when the telephone rang. Colonel Kaine from Chicago.

'We exchanged the usual greetings and then he said, "You can't play golf anywhere if you have financial pressures; how is your dollar situation?" Well, it was pretty bad, because dollars were difficult to get, legally or illegally. "In any case", he said, "where are you staying in Augusta?" I told him I had got rooms in a big pension and I gave him the name and address of the house and the telephone number.

'We went down to Augusta by night-train, hired a car and drove to this house, and on arrival I found an Express letter for me enclosing $1,000 from Colonel Kaine with affectionate regards, hoping it would help me cover some of my expenses. This meant I was now in his debt to the tune of $1,100.'

'The Masters finished. I did not play badly, and then I set off for the Westchester Country Club which is in Rye, New York State, having arranged with the Club's President, Vinny Ross, for Colonel Kaine to be a guest of mine in the Club's vast hotel where I had been magnanimously given member's privileges. I arranged to meet the Colonel at Rye Station, New York, on the electric commuter line from the big city.

'It was rather like Livingstone and Stanley. We had never met but he knew me from magazine photographs. I looked up and down the platform, which was almost deserted. Then at the far end of the train I saw a small fellow get out with a little canvas golf bag and a grip. I had not seen anybody else with a golf bag but had been expecting a huge American-type bag. I chanced it and walked down the platform, and as soon as we got within a few yards of one another he said, "Henry!" and I said "Colonel!" and we shook hands.

124

'I asked "Where is your luggage?" He replied, "I have no luggage, my boy, this is all I have. Take a tip from me, never own anything. This is all I have in the world."

'I had booked the Colonel Room 807 at the club and immediately we reached the lobby he went straight to the head porter and handed him $100, saying, "Colonel Kaine, 807, look after me." Then he marched to the telephone exchange, asked for the head girl, and told her, "I am Colonel Kaine, Room 807. When I call from the eighth floor give me a quick connection; got no time, no time left. I am a busy man", and he gave her $100.

'Next it was the turn of the fellow in charge of the elevator boys: "Here is $100. When I press the button on the eighth floor, come right up. I am a busy man and have no time." And so it went on — a tour of the hotel handing out a small fortune in $100 tips to ensure good service.

'The Colonel's little grip contained two bottles of Rye whisky, toilet things and a pair of bedroom slippers; nothing else. So I queried, "Where are your clothes?" He retorted, "I am about to fix that now!" He picked up the telephone and said, "Put me through to the best men's outfitting shop in Rye", and within seconds he was saying, "Here is Colonel Kaine, Room 807, Westchester Country Club, I want...[and he recited a list of clothing — underpants, socks, golf shoes, belts, suits, sweaters, shorts — he knew all the model numbers and sizes by heart]. Charge it to me." He next telephoned the best radio shop in town, to order a record player, two albums of Mantovani's restful music, and two television sets of a certain model and certain size. (He hated commercials and switched off the sound when they came on.) Several bottles of his favourite whisky were next on the order list, then he called the golf shop and said, "I am here for three weeks, name Colonel Kaine. I want six dozen Titlists in a ball bag, take the wrappers off. Always keep them clean for me and when they are showing signs of a bit of wear, change them and put some new ones in, charge Room 807."

'I thought, now what have I let myself in for? I have guaranteed him and I do not really know who he is. So I had a few inquiries made and learned that he was a Vice-President of the First National City Bank of Chicago. It was an enormous operation and he was in charge of property and loans. He lived for golf. He lived in the Chicago Athletic Club in one room in the summer and in the Edgewater Golf Hotel, Mississippi, in the winter. He went from one address to the other and when he left, or when he arrived, he went through the same performance. He gave everything away when he left and bought a new lot on arrival; that was what he meant when he said "Do not own anything". So he really travelled light.

'I said to him, "Colonel, what is the idea of giving all these tips before you get any service?" He replied, "Boy, remember this, get them on the team. They will be waiting all the rest of the stay for another tip." This rather impressed me and I have never forgotten his motto.

'The following morning we had arranged to meet at a quarter to nine. The bell captain rushed forward to tell me, "The Colonel is outside, he has gone for a walk, he will be back in just a few minutes." So I waited and suddenly he appeared. He pulled a pedometer from the watch pocket in his slacks and said, "Twelve hundred yards", and set off down the road again for another five hundred yards. "Now we go and practise", he said, having done more or less his after-breakfast mile.

'We went to the practice ground, but as soon as I saw him hit the ball, by the sound of the balls on the club and by the different directions they took, I realized his hands were gone, and sure enough they were arthritic. Just my luck, I thought, he cannot even hold the club!

'The accent in my teaching is always on the hands and it was obvious that there was not much I could do for the Colonel till he could hold on. So I got an adjustable bar for him, fixed it up across the entrance to the bathroom and got him to hang on it every day, despite the excruciating pain!

126

Gradually as his hands became a little stronger so his game improved, and two weeks later he was knocking the ball quite decently. Then his stay came to an end. He was very pleased with what I had done for him and showed it with a lot more dollars. As he started giving away everything he had acquired he said, "What would you like, Henry?" I thought to myself, I do not want radio or television sets, so I said, "Let me have the record player and the records".

The Colonel gave away the T.V.s, all his clothes, some of which he had not even put on, his shoes, the lot! Then I drove him to the station and put him back on the commuter train to New York where he took the train for Chicago, with just his canvas golf bag and grip.

'As I was leaving he said, "Have you got a motor car?" "Yes", I replied, "I have a car in England". He said, "What have you got?" I told him. "I will have a decent car sent to the docks and ship it to England to you", he said.

'He sent me a Lincoln, which I ran for a number of years, and it was always a reminder of this extraordinary fellow and his unusual advice, full of common sense!'